Naturally,
DELICIOUS
DANNY SEO

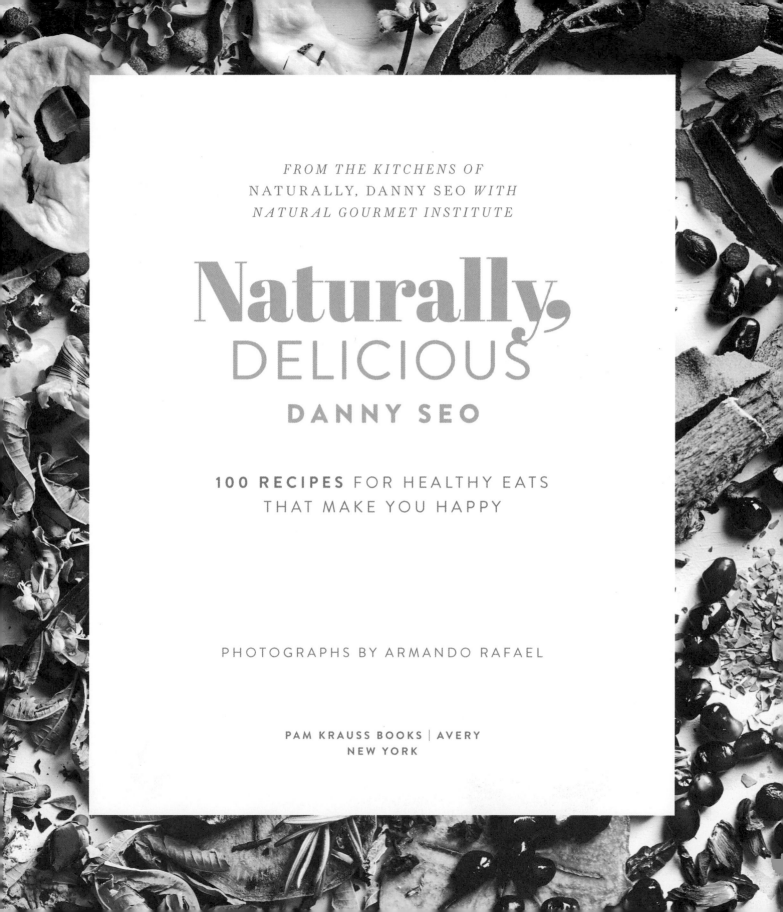

FROM THE KITCHENS OF
NATURALLY, DANNY SEO *WITH*
NATURAL GOURMET INSTITUTE

Naturally,
DELICIOUS

DANNY SEO

100 RECIPES FOR HEALTHY EATS
THAT MAKE YOU HAPPY

PHOTOGRAPHS BY ARMANDO RAFAEL

PAM KRAUSS BOOKS | AVERY
NEW YORK

Pam Krauss Books | Avery
an imprint of Penguin Random House LLC
375 Hudson Street
New York, New York 10014

Copyright © 2016 by Danny Seo Media Ventures

ISBN 9781101905302

Printed in China
1 3 5 7 9 10 8 6 4 2

Book and jacket design by Alexis Cook

Photograph on p. 126 by David Englehardt

All other photographs by Armando Rafael

For all those who help bring *Naturally, Danny Seo* to life with each and every issue.

CONTENTS

FOREWORD

I receive numerous cookbooks,
nutrition books, health books, and
medical textbooks to review
frequently. If I'm really
honest, that's not the part of
my job I typically enjoy.

While some photos or recipes in these books might be great, or I'll be impressed by the way a colleague communicates a health concept, I rarely feel that the new offerings will do much to help my patients—help people like *you*—get better health. I typically find books are lacking truly actionable tips or sufficient information to help readers customize advice. Not only is it not personal enough for different folks, but it's typically not personal enough for the *same* reader to glean info that'll work for them throughout their week, month, and even lives. Essentially, most books don't help us simplify better nutrition (which includes quality, quantity, nutrient balance, and frequency) to help get better health from our food choices.

When Danny asked me to read his cookbook manuscript, I jumped at the opportunity. I wanted his recipes, tips, and stories *for myself,* and had a feeling I would want to share them with my patients, colleagues, and friends. The same way I dive into his magazine, *Naturally, Danny Seo,* I dove into the manuscript. I found myself laughing out loud starting at page one and appreciated his honesty (you've got to love an author who outright admits that he's not a cooking expert but, instead, teamed up with the best). Then, I began to read the recipes and so began the mouth-watering . . .

Danny and his cookbook team deliver recipes—I made several within the first weeks of receiving this book, which, I'll be honest, *never happens.* I could go on about the *better nutrition* wins the recipes offer, but I wouldn't want to taint any of them with the "it's healthy" or "it's good for you" mentions that can deduct from excitement for and appreciation of their great taste. Of course the cookbook *naturally* includes Danny's tips, so you'll not only enjoy a variety of great-tasting food, but you will also glean resource-saving advice, and likely have a laugh or two.

I'm so glad you are reading this book. I'm so glad that Danny created it for all of us. Read on and bite into better nutrition to experience just how delicious better health tastes. Sorry! I had to! I'm a dietitian; it's my professional obligation to at least once mention how your food choices can deliver the better health we all crave. Happily, to satisfy that craving, all you have to do is make any of these recipes. Now that's *Better Nutrition, Simplified*!

Ashley Koff, RD
The *Better Nutrition, Simplified* Program

INTRODUCTION

It's confession time and here it is: I do not love to cook. That's right, the cookbook you are holding was written by someone who would rather spend his time just about anywhere else but in the kitchen. And that's where we may see eye-to-eye: I don't love to cook, but I do love to eat really delicious food.

It's no different from how I feel about exercise. I do not love huffing and puffing on the treadmill, but I like the endorphin rush and euphoric feeling I get when I'm done. And most of us find household chores like washing windows, scrubbing toilets, and vacuuming floors to be more drudgery than fun, right? But who doesn't like the end result: a clean, sparkling home?

But back to cooking . . .

I have friends who tell me they find pleasure—even joy—in cooking at home. Lucky them. To me, cooking feels like a homework assignment: gathering the ingredients, hunting for the right tools, and then devoting time and energy to bringing all those elements together in an attempt to produce something that tastes good enough to justify the effort. Unfortunately the alternative isn't very appealing,

either; a frozen organic burrito may be a timesaver, but the result is something less than palatable. So I've resigned myself to cooking in order to ensure that what I eat is not only good but also good *for* me. And while I may never learn to love cooking, I really do love everything that comes out of my kitchen these days—and I hope you will, too.

At the end of the day, my philosophy about food is pretty simple, and something that I think most cooks can relate to. Whether I'm cooking for myself or for a group, I want the recipes I tackle to be foolproof. And healthy. And delicious. And not dumbed down to where I'm serving toast smeared with mashed avocado and topped with freshly cracked peppercorns as supper. I don't need to roast a suckling pig or bone a duck at home to prove my worthiness in the kitchen, but let's not pretend I'm completely helpless either, okay?

When I created my magazine, *Naturally, Danny Seo*, food was a big part of the publication's editorial arc in my efforts to look at eco-friendly, healthy living from a modern point of view. Forget being preachy. Food is personal, and I did not want to create a forum for pitting vegans against meat eaters. The reality is that healthy eating has become the norm—not the exception—for the way we want to eat, but we all define for ourselves what eating healthy means. Your Paleo diet may not work for someone on a raw vegan plan—but you know what? That's just fine. Nowhere is the adage "to each his own" more apt than in the kitchen. What we do have in common is taste. We don't want food that tastes good; we want it to be *great*.

In the pages of *Naturally*, we look at the whole spectrum of good-for-you food and let readers decide, "Yes, this recipe works for me." But I also wanted to maintain the pleasure that comes from eating really good food; "healthy" shouldn't mean it has the appeal of wet cardboard. What about using real, wholesome ingredients that we intuitively know to be better for us, and that result in some pretty delicious grub? Forget calories or nutritional information; let's allow our intuition and inner voice to guide us toward real food that's really good for us. Our version of healthy makes plenty of room for creamy desserts, crunchy snacks, and all kinds of ooey-gooey goodness served piping hot from the oven.

Because I am not myself a chef, it was important to me to find just the right partners to work with to create the recipes for the magazine, and for this, our first-ever cookbook—and with the Natural Gourmet Institute (NGI) in New York City, we hit the jackpot. This leading culinary school trains everyone from serious chefs to home cooks who want to learn how to cook well-rounded, nutritious food. I've taken classes at NGI—such as a two-hour class on making Indian breads from scratch—which resulted in delicious success. Every recipe of theirs that we've featured in the pages of the magazine—from vegan ice cream made from cauliflower to fast and fresh paella—has worked. Perfectly.

These recipes will teach you new techniques and new ways to use ingredients you may not be familiar with. Each one is worth the time and effort. As cliché as it sounds, if *I* can do it (and *want* to do it), you can, too.

As I have just said, food is personal. Food is sensual. And food is something we can all be passionate about. Whether you're vegan, vegetarian, semi-vegetarian, Paleo, gluten free, raw only, or a meat eater who harbors caveman tendencies, you'll find a treasure trove of recipes and ideas in this book. Every diet, palate, or food like and dislike is welcome here. I don't eat meat, for example, but that's my choice. If you and your family or guests do, you will find dishes that my meat-eating friends gobbled up and agreed were delicious.

From the kitchens of *Naturally, Danny Seo*, we present our very first cookbook: *Naturally, Delicious*. I truly believe you will find this cookbook to be a natural addition to your home kitchen.

THE
NATURALLY, PERFECT
KITCHEN

I have an unusual approach to stocking my kitchen:
I pretend there could be a 24-hour blackout at any given time.
I think it has come from living in rural Pennsylvania, where
electrical outages are common whenever there is the slightest
rumbling of a storm. So, I've learned the hard (and expensive)
way to keep whatever is perishable to a minimum.

But over time, this anti-food hoarding mentality has helped me realize that buying
fresh, in-stock, and seasonally leads to a more diverse palette of food. If my go-to
veggies and proteins aren't available at my farmer's market, it leads me to try and
discover new things.

That said, my kitchen isn't bare bones. So, when stocking the *Naturally, Delicious*
kitchen, I have a few eco-tricks up my sleeve I want to share with you.

In the Pantry

HEALTHY OILS

I used to make a terrible mistake: I'd keep pricey jars of cooking and dressing oils right on the kitchen counter. But once you pop open the jars, the three things that can ruin them are oxygen (check!), light (sunny kitchen, check!), and heat (kept it right by stove, check!). One easy trick is to find organic oils that are packaged in opaque containers; this blocks the light from deteriorating the oil. But the easiest trick is to keep the pretty bottles of olive, avocado, and sunflower oil in the pantry, where it's cool and dark and they'll be happy.

HIMALAYAN ROCK SALT

Also known as "pink salt," Himalayan salt has a pretty fascinating story. Millions of years ago, crystallized sea salt beds were covered by lava. And these protected beds of salt ended up deep in the Himalayan mountains, shielded from pollution. Today, these salt caves are where you find the pink salt, and it's considered the purest form of salt you can find on Earth. It's also more than just tasty salt: it's loaded with 80+ minerals and completely unprocessed, unlike conventional table salt. I like the medium-size rock form and just run it across a hand-held grater for fresh salt dust to sprinkle on whatever needs a spike of salt.

ORGANIC HERBS AND SPICES

Whether it's ground turmeric, dried rosemary, or fennel seeds, all the seasonings in my spice rack are organic. Conventional dried herbs and spices are grown with chemical fertilizers and pesticides and are often irradiated to kill bacteria. Organic herbs and spices, on the other hand, are cultivated without chemicals and rid of pests and germs through steam heat or a deep freeze.

QUINOA

Quinoa has become my go-to starch to use as a base for stews, sautéed vegetables, fried tofu, or whenever I just need something a bit more to add to a dish to turn it from side idea into entrée. There has been controversy regarding quinoa. Given the rising popularity of the naturally gluten-free grain, it's driven up the prices, which some believe have forced families in poorer countries that grow quinoa (like Peru) deeper into poverty. So, one way to combat this is to look for Fair Trade quinoa, which empowers farms with increased wages, land ownership, and access to things like technology and education. I look for Fair Trade Certified quinoa, which is stamped on brands such as AlterEco.

GLUTEN-FREE PASTAS

There are so many varieties of gluten-free pasta now in the supermarket, it can be overwhelming. I like to stick with brown rice pastas that come in more durable shapes, like elbow and fusilli, instead of spaghetti style, which tends to break down easily in the cooking process. You can also find bean-based pastas made from soy, black, and mung beans, although it's a personal preference if you like the taste or not. These pastas tend to do better on their own, tossed with veggies, protein, and a dash of soy sauce.

CARTONS OF TOMATOES

Canned tomatoes are convenient, but recent controversies over the use of BPA-lined cans has many companies rushing to release BPA-free cans. Since tomatoes are highly acidic, even BPA-free cans still have to use some kind of chemical to prevent spoilage inside the can. I think the best solution is to look for tomatoes that are packaged in Tetra Paks or in glass jars. You can find them at the health food store, and they are great to have on hand for soups, stews, and sauces when tomatoes aren't in season.

BULK BIN GRAINS AND LEGUMES

Buying scoops of ingredients from the bulk bin isn't just more environmentally-friendly, it's also about 89 percent cheaper in overall cost, according to a 2012 study from Portland State University. So, I'll use the bins to get things I don't eat on a frequent basis but are helpful to have on hand in case I (or my guests) get the munchies. Bulk popcorn is great to have, so I'll buy a few scoops and store the kernels in glass canning jars. Other things I tend to pick up in the bulk aisles include beans of any kinds, including garbanzos and lentils red, green, and brown; grains like farro, millet, amaranth, barley, and rices long- and short-grained; and spices I use infrequently and that would lose potency before I used up a big jar.

NATURALLY, SWEET

Sure, sugar comes from the sugarcane plant, but it's something you should avoid altogether. Most sugar is grown with fertilizers and insecticides, and when it's ready to harvest, they burn the fields to remove the unproductive leafy matter on the plant. It's. Just. Terrible. I prefer naturally sweet alternatives like locally harvested honey, coconut sugar, grade B organic maple syrup, and organic agave syrup. Even if you have just one of these sweeteners handy, you should be fine in making almost any of the recipes in this book.

In the Fridge

EGGS

Never buy eggs from a supermarket. Doesn't matter if they're conventional, organic, or free-range, the reality is most of those eggs are at least 21 days old before they make it to your grocery store. Instead, try to buy locally grown eggs. Here's why: these chickens are likely roaming free around a yard, eating whatever they really find tasty like bugs and seeds (in addition to non-GMO feed they are likely eating, too). So, when chickens eat what they find tasty, it leads to better-tasting eggs. And eggs that are days (even hours) old when they reach you have a huge difference in taste than supermarket eggs. I'm lucky enough to have a neighbor (I call her "The Chicken Lady") where I put $3 in a coffee tin and grab a dozen eggs out of the henhouse. If that isn't in your neighborhood, look for fresh eggs at farmers markets or health food stores. And you can stock up. The trick is to lightly coat eggs you aren't using right away with vegetable oil. Egg shells are porous and will dry out what's inside very slowly over time, so the oil creates a barrier that protects and prolongs your eggs.

SOY OR ALMOND MILK

I remember when I was a teenage vegan, there really was just one choice of non-dairy milk. And it wasn't very good. Today is a whole different story with soy, almond, cashew, and coconut milks flooding the marketplace. Choose whatever flavor you like best, but always go with the choice that has the least amount of sugar. When you make anything with soy or nut milks, you can always add sweetener instead of vice versa.

ORGANIC MILK

Conventional dairy milk can be loaded with synthetic hormones and antibiotics, so it makes sense to choose organic milk. Even though organic milk costs more, in the long run, organic milk actually saves you money. You see, organic milk is sterilized at a higher temperature than regular milk—280°F vs. 145°F—so the shelf life is around two months (about double regular milk). If nut milks aren't your thing, this is the next best thing.

UNREFINED VIRGIN COCONUT OIL

Coconut oil can be expensive, so if you find a great deal, go ahead and stock up. It has a shelf life of two years, making it a very long-lasting cooking oil. The reason I keep jars of coconut oil in the fridge is that it turns into liquid at a cool 76 degrees. So in the summer months, it can go from spreadable paste to liquid even in an air-conditioned home. When it's in a solid, paste-y form, it's easier to measure vs. eyeballing it when it's liquefied (although no nutritional harm is done if the coconut oil does liquefy).

BROWN RICE

It's common knowledge that brown rice is more nutritious than white rice. Since the hulls and brans in brown rice haven't been stripped away, it's loaded with natural proteins and fiber and vitamins like calcium, magnesium, and potassium. But since the rice bran oil hasn't been stripped away, brown rice can go rancid quickly in the pantry. I keep it stored in my refrigerator, where the cooler temps double the shelf life from three months to six.

CHIA, FLAX, AND HEMP SEEDS

There are loads of nutritional seeds a lot of us are buying to toss into smoothies, sprinkle onto salads, and add as a nutritional boost to whatever we're cooking or eating. The problem is most seeds come in plastic pouches, which don't do a really good job of resealing once you've ripped one open. I transfer seeds to glass canning jars and store them in the fridge. It'll keep the seeds fresh for one year, and many nutritionists believe the nutritional content of the seeds will be higher than if kept at room temperature.

APPLES

Fall season is apple-picking time where I live in Pennsylvania. But leaving fresh apples on the kitchen counter can lead to spoiled fruit in as little as two days. Here's a trick I learned from the orchard owners: wrap each apple in a small square of newspaper. Wrapping the apple in newspaper helps prevent them from bruising one another, which speeds up the ripening process and turns fresh apples into rotten ones very quickly. After wrapping each apple, place them in a storage container in the fridge. They'll last for several weeks.

In the Freezer

FLOURS

I don't do a whole lot of baking, so when I do buy flour, it tends to last a very long time. I keep three types of flour in my kitchen—whole wheat, coconut, and a gluten-free 1-for-1 variety by Bob's Red Mill. When I open the bags, I immediately transfer the contents to an airtight container and keep them stored in the freezer. If you keep flour in the freezer, it can last indefinitely according to the Wheat Foods Council. In the fridge, you've two whole years.

PRE-WASHED GREENS

I love to buy bags of pre-washed organic greens like chopped kale, spinach, and baby lettuces and just toss them right into the freezer. These greens have been triple washed and are spun dry, so they freeze up without clumping together. Then when I make smoothies I'll throw a handful of frozen greens into the blender which gives it just enough of a chill. Added bonus: freezing greens prevents the multiplication of harmful bacteria, which is not true if left in the fridge.

SEASONAL BERRIES

There's nothing worse than fresh berries in the middle of winter: they are mealy, tough, juice-less, and just, blah. When berries are in season (and at their cheapest), take the time to wash, cut, and freeze them on unbleached parchment–lined baking sheets. And when they are fully frozen, transfer them to freezer bags so they're ready to toss into smoothies or warmed up with maple syrup to top freshly made French toast when Old Man Winter comes storming in.

ICE CUBES

I make my own ice cubes at home using silicone ice cube trays and not an automatic ice cube maker. The reason? I find even filtered water can result in cloudy cubes that can still leave a lingering aftertaste in drinks. Making "artisanal" cubes is a cinch: I first boil water in a kettle and allow it to cool down for a few minutes. Then I pour the water into silicone ice cube trays and pop them into the freezer. When I use boiled water, I end up with crystal-clear cubes with zero aftertaste.

Tools

FOOD WRAPS

Many plastic wraps are made from polyvinyl chloride (PVC), which is a known endocrine disrupter. But even with new PVC-free wraps coming to market, I just feel better not having a non-recyclable plastic covering my food. As an alternative, I use a beeswax-soaked fabric called Beeswrap, which works just like plastic wrap and can cover bowls, cut fruit, cheese, bread, whatever you want to cover. The unbleached fabric is dipped in a mix of melted beeswax, resin, and jojoba oil (which makes it anti-microbial) and the heat of your hand melds it into shape. Just rinse it under cold water and you can use it for around one year per wrap.

GLASS CONTAINERS

For food storage containers, glass is the only way to go. Unlike plastic, glass is non-porous, is microwave-safe, and won't get stained or retain odors. I like glass containers that also have a matching glass lid (found mine at Ikea). An alternative is to put leftovers in a ceramic bowl and invert a small ceramic plate on top to act as a lid. It does the trick pretty well.

COMMERCIAL-GRADE PLASTIC CONTAINERS

When I make my own lunch and bring it to work, glass is impractical. So, I use these BPA-free, commercial-grade takeout containers that mimic the look of Styrofoam disposables, but in an eco-friendly reusable way. The compartments keep ingredients separate, and it's translucent, so you can see right inside. Called "Eco Takeouts" (you can find them online), they were originally made for college campuses where disposables were banned. They are dishwasher safe for thousands of times in a commercial dishwasher, so they are pretty much indestructible at home. I even bring them to restaurants to use for my leftovers because they hold up much better than flimsy foam and paper.

SILICONE ICE CUBE TRAYS

The reason I choose silicone trays over old-fashioned plastic ones is that plastic can leach the chemical BPA into the cubes. Silicone, on the other hand, is sterile and has zero chance of chemical leaching. Plus, silicone trays come in all sorts of fun shapes and sizes to make pretty cool cubes.

UNBLEACHED PARCHMENT AND RECYCLED ALUMINUM FOIL

There is absolutely zero benefit from cooking on white parchment paper, which has been bleached with chlorine. Unbleached parchment works equally as well. When it comes to aluminum foil, go with 100 percent recycled aluminum, which works just as well as virgin ore foil. Plus, it's still recyclable in your own curbside recycling bin.

BROWN PAPER LUNCH BAGS

Yes, the lunch sacks your mother sent you to school with are great to have on hand. For this cookbook's shaking/baking recipes, for making microwave popcorn at home, and for a whole host of other reasons, a pack of 100 bags is always handy to have stashed away in the drawer.

METAL TEA BALLS AND STRAINERS

Sure, prefilled tea bags are convenient, but did you know many of them are made with a thermoplastic or bleached paper filter? When you pour boiling-hot water over these bags, there is a risk of polymers or bleaching chemicals leaching into your hot cup of oolong. The fact is, buying loose tea and filling your own stainless steel balls and strainers is pretty easy to do and saves you money, too. But it also allows you to customize flavors by mixing different teas together to make your own custom brew at home.

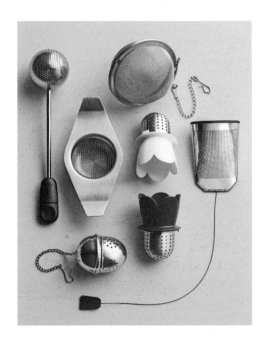

CHAPTER ONE

weekend recharge

Many people are surprised to learn I call a small river town in rural Bucks County, Pennsylvania, home. My 1920s craftsman cabin sits high above the Delaware River, bare of what I call "digital distractions." No Wi-Fi, no cable TV, no cell service—not even a landline. When I come home from a photo shoot half-way around the world, a marathon of meetings in my magazine's New York City office, or from filming television segments, the moment I set foot through the door it's a respite from what can feel like a slightly chaotic world. I've purposefully de-modernized my life to early 2000 standards.

The downside of this bucolic refuge is my commute, which entails catching at 5 a.m. the single New York City–bound bus that serves my area. That morning routine omits the possibility of whipping up a fanciful breakfast. Come Saturday, though, it's a different story. I often have guests who get their best sleep ever in the pitch-black, whisper-quiet nights of my home. And when they finally awaken, they are *hungry*.

I lean toward crowd-pleasers like pancakes, waffles, and frittatas that are fast and easy to make. These fuel our adventures at the local flea markets, along the hiking trails, or (I am not joking here) at the vast, clean, modern store my New York City friends call "Suburban Target." Whatever lies in store for you and your guests this weekend, even if it's just tackling a mountain of chores, making any of these Instagram-worthy recipes won't feel like one of those chores.

ACTIVE TIME 40 MINUTES
TOTAL TIME 40 MINUTES
MAKES 8 PANCAKES
SERVES 4

SAVORY TURMERIC PANCAKES WITH LEMON YOGURT SAUCE

Turmeric is the new kale. That is, it's the new superfood that you'll be seeing *everywhere* soon. It is one of the most powerful anti-inflammatory ingredients you can use, but it's gentle on the stomach, inexpensive, and easy to find. You can buy turmeric fresh (a rhizome, it looks like a skinnier fresh gingerroot), but powdered turmeric is just fine and is easier to work with. I love the bright, vibrant orange color that turmeric gives these pancakes. They aren't like the light and fluffy buttermilk-type pancake; these are dense, thick, and loaded with filling. Two of these guys are a *meal*.

This recipe is gluten-free, but feel free to swap out the almond flour for whole wheat if gluten is not a concern.

FOR THE YOGURT SAUCE

1 cup plain Greek yogurt
1 garlic clove, minced
1 to 2 tablespoons lemon juice
  (from 1 lemon), to taste
¼ teaspoon ground turmeric
10 fresh mint leaves, minced
2 teaspoons lemon zest (from 1 lemon)

FOR THE PANCAKES

2 teaspoons ground turmeric
1½ teaspoons ground cumin
1 teaspoon salt
1 teaspoon ground coriander
½ teaspoon garlic powder
½ teaspoon freshly ground black pepper
1 head broccoli, cut into florets
3 large eggs, lightly beaten
2 tablespoons plain unsweetened
  almond milk
1 cup almond flour
4 teaspoons coconut oil

1. Make the yogurt sauce. Combine the yogurt, garlic, lemon juice, turmeric, mint, and zest in a bowl. Taste and season with more lemon juice, if needed. Set aside or refrigerate until ready to serve.

2. Make the pancakes. In a small bowl, combine the turmeric, cumin, salt, coriander, garlic, and pepper.

3. Place the broccoli in a food processor, and pulse until the florets are broken up into small pieces. Transfer the broccoli to a large bowl and add the eggs, almond milk, and almond flour. Stir in the spice mix and combine well.

4. Heat 1 teaspoon of the coconut oil in a nonstick pan over medium-low heat. Pour ¼ cup batter into the skillet. Cook the pancake until small bubbles begin to appear on the surface and the bottom is golden brown, 2 to 3 minutes. Flip over and cook the pancake for 2 to 3 minutes more. To keep warm, transfer the cooked pancakes to an oven-safe dish and place in a 200°F oven.

5. Continue making the remaining pancakes, using the remaining oil and batter.

SAVORY YOGURT BOWLS

One of the places I stay often is the Public Hotel, in Chicago. I call it the Goldilocks of hotels: everything about it is just right, from the design and the price, to the location and the food. The on-site farm-to-table restaurant, The Pump Room, was created by acclaimed chef Jean-Georges Vongerichten, but for me, the real deliciousness is in the takeout section across the lobby, in the library coffee bar. Jean-Georges also curated the bar's mix of to-go salads, sandwiches, and what I crave most: savory yogurts. Inspired by these flavorful cups, here are three easy-to-make yogurts *j'adore*.

YOGURT WITH BALSAMIC BEET PUREE SWIRL

ACTIVE TIME 15 MINUTES
TOTAL TIME 1 HOUR 15 MINUTES
SERVES 4

1 pound small beets, cleaned and trimmed
1 tablespoon balsamic vinegar
½ teaspoon salt
1 quart plain Greek yogurt

1. Preheat the oven to 400°F.

2. Wrap each beet tightly in aluminum foil and place on the middle oven rack. Roast for 1 hour, or until easily pierced with a fork. When the beets are cool enough to handle, peel off the skins and discard.

3. Cut the beets into 1-inch chunks and place in a food processor. Add the vinegar, salt, and 1 cup of the yogurt. Puree until smooth.

4. To serve, divide the remaining yogurt among the bowls and top each with some beet puree. If desired, swirl together with a spoon.

Do Ahead The beet puree can be prepared up to two days in advance and refrigerated until ready to serve.

SMOKED SALMON TOAST WITH KALE-DILL YOGURT

ACTIVE TIME 10 MINUTES
TOTAL TIME 10 MINUTES
SERVES 4

FOR THE YOGURT

1 cup plain Greek yogurt
Zest of ½ lemon
1 tablespoon fresh lemon juice
   (from 1 lemon)
2 tablespoons chopped fresh dill
½ cup baby kale
½ teaspoon Dijon mustard
Pinch of salt
Pinch of ground black pepper

FOR THE ASSEMBLY

4 slices whole-grain sandwich
   bread, toasted and cut into
   cubes
8 ounces thinly sliced smoked
   salmon, chopped
½ cup thinly sliced red onion
2 tablespoons drained capers
Dill sprigs, for garnish

1. Make the yogurt. In a food
   processor, combine the
   yogurt, lemon zest, lemon
   juice, dill, kale, salt, and
   pepper. Puree until smooth
   and transfer to a bowl.
   Cover and refrigerate until
   ready to serve.

2. To serve, spoon some of the
   yogurt, salmon, and toast
   cubes in layers into serving
   cups. Top each serving
   with some onion slices and
   capers, and garnish each
   with a dill sprig.

Do Ahead The kale-dill yogurt
can be prepared up to 24 hours
in advance and refrigerated
until ready to serve.

YOGURT WITH ROASTED CARROT PUREE SWIRL AND TOASTED WALNUTS

ACTIVE TIME 10 MINUTES
TOTAL TIME 35 MINUTES
SERVES 4

1 pound carrots, cut
   into ½-inch slices
1 tablespoon extra-
   virgin olive oil
¼ teaspoon ground
   nutmeg
¼ teaspoon ground
   cinnamon
½ teaspoon salt
¼ teaspoon ground
   black pepper
2 teaspoons lemon
   juice (from ½ lemon)
1 quart plain Greek
   yogurt
½ cup walnuts, toasted
   and chopped

1. Preheat the oven
   to 400°F. Line a
   rimmed baking
   sheet with parch-
   ment paper.

2. In a large bowl,
   toss together the
   carrots, olive oil,
   nutmeg, cinna-
   mon, salt, and
   pepper. Transfer
   to the prepared
   baking sheet and,
   in a single layer,
   roast until the
   carrot slices can
   easily be pierced
   with a fork, about
   30 minutes.

3. Transfer the
   carrots to a food
   processor. Add
   the lemon juice
   and 1 cup of the
   yogurt; puree
   until smooth.

4. To serve, divide
   the remaining
   yogurt among
   bowls and top
   each with some
   carrot puree.
   Swirl away. Sprin-
   kle with toasted
   walnuts.

Do Ahead The
carrot puree can be
prepared up to two
days in advance and
refrigerated until
ready to serve.

OVERNIGHT AMARANTH PORRIDGE WITH MANGO PUREE AND PISTACHIOS

I know, Porridge? Ewww. But just as Brussels sprouts can either be cooked to be mouthwateringly delicious or seriously disgusting, there is bad porridge and there is the warm, creamy, and comforting version. This guy is the latter.

Put this hot cereal in your slow cooker the night before a big snowstorm. When you wake up in the morning to the fluffy stuff all around you, you can spoon this into a bowl and have yourself a magical moment.

FOR THE CEREAL

1 tablespoon coconut oil

3 medium apples, cored and cut into 1-inch cubes

8 large Medjool dates, pitted and quartered

1½ teaspoons ground cinnamon

¼ teaspoon ground nutmeg

1½ teaspoons vanilla extract

2 tablespoons fresh orange juice (from ½ orange)

1 cup amaranth

½ cup plain unsweetened almond milk

1¼ cups water

FOR THE TOPPING

1 mango, pitted and peeled

½ cup shelled pistachios, chopped

1. Prepare the cereal. Grease the bottom and sides of a small slow cooker with the coconut oil. In layers, add the apples, dates, cinnamon, nutmeg, vanilla, orange juice, amaranth, and almond milk, in that order. Add the water, then cover and cook the porridge on low heat for 8 hours.

2. Make the topping. Slice the mango off the pit and set aside a few of the nicest slices for garnish. Place the remaining mango in a blender with a scant tablespoon of water. Puree the mango with the water until smooth.

3. Serve the porridge warm, topped with the mango puree and slices and a sprinkle of pistachios.

Do Ahead The mango puree can be prepared the night before as well, so as to be ready when the porridge is served.

Tip Almost all yogurt containers are stamped with a #5 recycling symbol on the bottom. In most communities, curbside programs accept #1 (clear plastics like soda bottles) and #2 (opaque bottles like laundry detergent), but rarely anything else. When it comes to recycling your yogurt containers, don't toss them into the recycling bin thinking, "Plastic is plastic, right?" When a load of recyclables gets contaminated with too many non-recyclable materials, the whole batch often is discarded into a landfill, rather than being sorted. Save your #5 plastic yogurt containers and bring them to a special "Gimme 5" recycling bin, often at stores like Whole Foods. They will then get recycled into new plastic products.

try these
7 GREAT-GREAT-GREAT GRAINS

SORGHUM
A.K.A.: Milo

Ancient Roots: First found 8,000 years ago in Southern Egypt.

Flavor: Neutral, sometimes sweet

Nutrition: Gluten-free; high in iron and fiber

How to Use It: Popped like popcorn; ground into flour for baking; cooked in porridge; brewed into gluten-free beer.

MILLET
A.K.A.: Birdseed—the small round seeds you've seen in a bird feeder

Ancient Roots: Appears in the Old Testament. Likely cultivated in Asia and Africa more than 7,000 years ago.

Flavor: Mildly sweet, nutty

Nutrition: Gluten-free; good source of protein; high in fiber, B vitamins, and magnesium

How to Use It: Ground into flour for baking; popped like popcorn; cooked and mixed with seasoned meats, veggies, and beans.

RYE
A.K.A.: The ingredient in the classic sandwich bread

Ancient Roots: In Central and Eastern Europe since medieval times; first appears as a cultivated crop around 1800–1500 B.C.

Flavor: Hearty, deep, rich

Nutrition: Lower in gluten than wheats; rich source of dietary fiber

How to Use It: Think beyond baking. Use cooked rye berries in side dishes, salads, and soups. You can also use rye for microbrewed beers.

KASHA
A.K.A.: Roasted buckwheat groats

Ancient Roots: China, as early as the 5th–3rd century B.C.

Flavor: Nutty

Nutrition: Gluten-free; ranks low on the glycemic scale; packed with protein

How to Use It: Popular as a hot or cold breakfast, kasha also makes a satisfying side dish or ingredient in a salad.

KAMUT®
A.K.A.: Khorasan wheat

Ancient Roots: This distant relative of modern wheat may have originated in King Tut's time in Egypt.

Flavor: Naturally sweet

Nutrition: Significantly higher protein than common wheat; high amounts of the antioxidant mineral selenium

How to Use It: Ground into flour for baking; cooked into stews, soups, and pilafs; in salads.

AMARANTH

A.K.A.: Pigweed
Ancient Roots: Cultivated by the Aztecs and the Incas; domesticated 6,000–8,000 years ago.
Flavor: Mildly nutty and peppery
Nutrition: Gluten-free and wheat-free; rich in protein and amino acids such as lysine
How to Use It: Popular breakfast porridge, amaranth can also be ground into a baking flour, used in soups and salads, or popped like popcorn.

RED LENTILS

A.K.A.: Masoor Dal
Ancient Roots: Seeds found in the Middle East date back to 6000 B.C. Appears in the Old Testament.
Flavor: Mild, slightly earthy
Nutrition: Gluten-free; high in protein and iron; good source of fiber
How to Use It: Red lentils—which tend to cook faster than other types of lentils—are perfect in stews, soups, purées, casseroles, and curries.

QUINOA PORRIDGE WITH ROASTED CHERRY TOMATOES, ARUGULA, AND MANCHEGO

This is the perfect Sunday brunch dish because it's delicious for breakfast or lunch, and it can be saved and reheated for late guests. I consider organic quinoa a go-to food when I'm "hangry" and am tempted simply to nuke a frozen breakfast burrito. As a plant-based complete protein, quinoa is loaded with good-for-you nutrients like iron, magnesium, calcium, and vitamins E and B. On the weekend, I make an extra-large batch of this porridge and store the leftovers; come Monday night, after a long day at the office, I'll heat some of it and put a fried egg on top for an instant dinner.

2 cups boiling water

1 cup quinoa, rinsed

Salt and freshly ground black pepper

2 pints cherry tomatoes

2 tablespoons extra-virgin olive oil

4 ounces Manchego cheese, grated

3 ounces baby arugula, roughly chopped

1. Preheat the oven to 400°F. Line a rimmed baking sheet with parchment paper.

2. In a small baking dish, combine the boiling water, quinoa, and ½ teaspoon salt. Cover tightly with foil and bake for 20 minutes.

3. On the prepared baking sheet, toss the cherry tomatoes with the olive oil and pinches of salt and pepper. Roast until the tomatoes are soft and slightly blistered, about 20 minutes.

4. In a large bowl, stir together the quinoa, tomatoes, the cheese, and half the arugula. Taste, and season with salt and pepper, if needed.

5. Garnish with the remaining arugula and serve.

Do Ahead This dish can be prepared one day in advance and kept in the fridge until ready to serve.

Tip If you find quinoa on sale in your market, stock up on it, as it can last in the pantry for up to three years. Similarly, cooked quinoa is fine for a few days in the refrigerator but can last up to a year in the freezer, which makes it the perfect make-ahead side dish.

BUCKWHEAT PORRIDGE WITH MUSHROOMS AND A FRIED EGG

You know how a tomato isn't really a vegetable—that it's botanically a fruit? Well, buckwheat isn't really a grain; it's a seed that comes from a fruit. So, for those of you with sensitivities to gluten, here's a really delicious gluten-free porridge that will have you thinking you're indulging in a big bowl of wheaty deliciousness.

Buckwheat is a miracle food: it's high in protein, naturally chemical free (does not need pesticides or insecticides to thrive, so you'll likely *only* ever find organic buckwheat), and has a mild taste that is well suited to both savory and sweet recipes.

1 cup water

2 cups plain unsweetened almond milk

Salt

1 cup raw buckwheat

2 tablespoons extra-virgin olive oil

1 medium onion, chopped (about 1 cup)

2 pounds mixed mushrooms, such as cremini, shiitake, and oyster, cleaned, stemmed, and sliced

1 garlic clove, chopped

½ teaspoon ground black pepper, plus more to taste

2 tablespoons butter

4 large eggs

2 tablespoons chopped fresh chives

1. In a medium saucepan, bring the water, almond milk, and ½ teaspoon salt to a boil over high heat. Stir in the buckwheat, turn the heat down to low, cover, and simmer for 10 minutes.

2. In a large saucepan, heat the olive oil over medium heat. Add the onion and cook until softened, about 5 minutes. Add the mushrooms and cook for 2 minutes without stirring. When the mushrooms are beginning to brown, stir and cook for 2 more minutes. Add the garlic, pepper, and ½ teaspoon salt, and cook for 1 more minute.

3. Stir the buckwheat into the mushroom mixture. Taste and season with salt, if necessary. Keep warm over low heat.

4. In a large nonstick or cast-iron skillet, melt the butter over medium heat. Crack the eggs into the skillet and turn the heat down to medium-low. Season with salt and pepper. Cook until the egg whites are set and the edges are crisp, about 4 minutes.

5. To serve, divide the porridge among serving bowls and top each with an egg; sprinkle with the chives.

Do Ahead The porridge can be prepared up to two days in advance and refrigerated, then reheated when ready to serve.

Tip Are you allergic to down feather pillows but would like a little natural support for your neck? Tuck into a bowl of buckwheat porridge, then tuck yourself in with a buckwheat pillow. Buckwheat hulls are used to fill pillows because they are naturally non-allergenic. The buckwheat hulls mold to the shape of your neck for support, and the extra bonus is that dust mites hate living in the hulls.

KALE, RED ONION, AND GOAT-CHEESE STRATA

Here's some one-pot deliciousness that even the most indifferent home cooks can whip up without failure. It uses what most of us already have in the fridge to yield something pretty gourmet—as if MacGyver had a show on the Food Network. I can see him whipping this up. In a jail cell. Surrounded by spies. While detonating a bomb.

2 tablespoons plus 1 teaspoon extra-virgin olive oil

Zest of 1 lemon

2 teaspoons Dijon mustard

½ teaspoon salt

¼ teaspoon black pepper

2 cups plain unsweetened almond milk

6 large eggs

4 slices whole wheat sandwich bread, cut into ½-inch cubes (about 3 cups)

2 cups packed baby kale, roughly chopped

1 small red onion, thinly sliced

½ cup crumbled goat cheese

1. Preheat the oven to 400°F. Grease a 9-inch round baking dish with 1 teaspoon of the olive oil.

2. In a medium bowl, whisk together the lemon zest, mustard, salt, pepper, almond milk, eggs, and remaining 2 tablespoons olive oil.

3. In a large bowl, combine the bread cubes, kale, onion, and half the goat cheese. Gently toss with your hands and transfer to the prepared baking dish.

4. Pour the egg mixture into the dish, making sure all ingredients are evenly covered. Top with the remaining ¼ cup goat cheese. Bake until the center of the strata is no longer jiggly and the edges are browned, about 1 hour. Serve warm.

Tip Buckwheat flour does not have a long shelf life (about two months), so if you don't plan on using it regularly, it's best to buy just what you need from the bulk bin section of your market. If you can't find it in the bulk section, you can store unused packaged buck-wheat flour in an airtight container in the freezer, where it can stay fresh for six months.

BUCKWHEAT PANCAKES WITH SAUTÉED CINNAMON APPLE

We chose an apple for the fruit topping here because they are available year-round, but feel free to use any seasonal fruit that calls to you. Also, if you are watching your sugar intake, it's worth trying to get your hands on coconut sugar. It's made simply by heating the sap from the coconut palm until the water evaporates. It's delicious, and many nutritionists and doctors agree that it does not spike blood sugar levels as refined white sugar does.

If you prefer "silver dollar" pancakes to the traditional plate size, use only 2 tablespoons of batter per pancake.

FOR THE CINNAMON APPLE

1 apple, peeled, cored, and thinly sliced
½ teaspoon ground cinnamon
1 teaspoon coconut sugar or turbinado sugar
1 teaspoon coconut oil

FOR THE PANCAKES

1 cup buckwheat flour
½ teaspoon baking powder
1 teaspoon coconut sugar or turbinado sugar
¼ teaspoon ground cardamom
1 banana, peeled and mashed
½ teaspoon vanilla extract
1½ cups plain unsweetened almond milk,
  at room temperature
2 tablespoons coconut oil, plus more
  for cooking
Grade B organic maple syrup, for serving

1. Make the cinnamon apple. In a bowl, combine the apple, cinnamon, and sugar; toss to coat.

2. Heat the coconut oil in a small nonstick skillet over medium-low heat. Add the apple and sauté until softened and caramelized, 15 to 20 minutes.

3. Make the pancakes. In a large bowl, whisk together the flour, baking powder, sugar, and cardamom. In a separate bowl, combine the banana, vanilla, almond milk, and coconut oil.

4. Fold the banana mixture into the flour mixture and stir until smooth. If the batter seems too thin, stir in a bit more flour; if too thick, add a little milk.

5. Heat 1 teaspoon coconut oil in a nonstick skillet (or grease a griddle, if you have one) over medium heat. Scoop ¼ cup of batter into the skillet and cook until bubbles appear on the surface, about 3 minutes. Flip and cook until the pancake moves freely in the pan, 2 to 3 minutes. Transfer to a platter and continue making pancakes with the remaining batter, adding more coconut oil to the skillet as needed.

6. Serve the pancakes topped with the cinnamon apple and a drizzle of maple syrup.

Do Ahead The cinnamon apple mixture can be made one day ahead and refrigerated; reheat the apple mixture before serving.

BAKED PEACH FRENCH TOAST WITH BERRY-FIG COMPOTE

French toast cooked in a standard frying pan with lots of butter can be a greasy mess. But French toast baked in the oven is a light, crispy feat of breakfast marvelousness.

If you've made the Honey-Spelt Loaf (page 101), any leftover slices are beautiful in this recipe. But, really, any type of leftover bread works well. Depending on whether you use fresh or frozen berries, you'll want to adjust the amount of maple syrup and lemon juice. Start with less syrup and add more as needed.

FOR THE FRENCH TOAST

1½ cups plain unsweetened almond milk

3 large eggs

2 tablespoons grade B organic maple syrup

1 teaspoon vanilla extract

½ teaspoon ground cinnamon

8 slices bread of choice

2 small peaches, halved and thinly sliced

FOR THE BERRY-FIG COMPOTE

1½ cups blueberries, fresh or frozen

8 fresh figs, halved

2 to 3 tablespoons grade B organic
   maple syrup

1 to 2 tablespoons lemon juice
   (from 1 lemon)

1. Make the French toast. Preheat the oven to 400°F. In a medium bowl, whisk together the almond milk, eggs, maple syrup, vanilla, and cinnamon.

2. Line the bottom of an 8-inch square baking dish with 4 slices of the bread—you may squish them together to fit. Arrange the peaches on top in an even layer. Pour half the milk mixture over the bread and peaches. Layer the remaining 4 bread slices over the peaches, and cover with the remaining milk mixture. Using a spatula, press down to saturate the bread.

3. Cover the dish with aluminum foil and bake for 20 minutes. Uncover and bake until set and top is golden brown, about 10 minutes more.

4. Make the berry-fig compote and assemble. In a medium pot over medium-high heat, combine the blueberries, figs, maple syrup, and lemon juice. Bring to a boil, stirring often, then reduce the heat to low. Simmer for 15 to 20 minutes. The fruit will break down and create a thick syrup.

5. Place servings of the French toast on plates and top with the compote.

Tip Want to save money when shopping for organic frozen fruits and vegetables? Look for store brands instead of national brands. The store brands are less expensive but follow the same USDA standards.

SAVORY CHICKPEA WAFFLES WITH MAPLE SYRUP AND SHIITAKE CRUMBLE

Anyone who has stayed at a large chain hotel has likely encountered the free continental breakfast in the lobby with a DIY waffle station anchoring the whole setup. I like to watch businessmen attempting, from what I can gather, to "cook" for the first time. Batter goes in. Batter goes everywhere else as well. The waffles fail to come to fruition. But they try and try again, and eventually—voilà! They get their waffles. Crispy, light, cakey.

When I have guests staying overnight, I do a fancy version of the Hampton Inn free breakfast: I pre-mix the batter, grease the waffle maker, and even plug it in for them so they can tell their co-workers Monday that they, too, "cooked."

FOR THE SHIITAKE CRUMBLE

1 pound fresh shiitake mushrooms, stemmed
2 tablespoons extra-virgin olive oil
Pinch of salt

FOR THE WAFFLES

1½ cups chickpea flour
2 teaspoons baking powder
¼ teaspoon baking soda
½ teaspoon salt
½ teaspoon ground cinnamon
2 tablespoons turbinado sugar
  or coconut sugar
1½ cups plain unsweetened almond milk
2 large eggs
¼ cup coconut oil, melted
Cooking spray

FOR SERVING

Crème fraîche or sour cream
Grade B organic maple syrup

1. Make the shiitake crumble. Preheat the oven to 325°F. In a food processor, pulse the shiitake mushrooms until they are minced.

2. Spread the minced mushrooms on a parchment-lined baking sheet, drizzle with the olive oil, and sprinkle with the salt. Toss to combine. Bake until crisp, about 30 minutes, tossing once with a spatula after 15 minutes. Transfer to a bowl to cool.

3. Make the waffles. Preheat a waffle iron. In a large bowl, whisk together the chickpea flour, baking powder, baking soda, salt, cinnamon, and sugar. Make a well in the center and pour in the almond milk, eggs, and coconut oil. Whisk together to make a thin batter.

4. Coat the waffle iron with cooking spray, then pour in a quarter of the batter and cook the waffle according to the manufacturer's directions, until browned and there's no steam coming from the iron's edges. Remove the waffle and continue to make remaining waffles. Cooked waffles may be kept warm in a 200°F oven.

5. Serve the warm waffles topped with a dollop of crème fraîche or sour cream, sprinkled with shiitake crumble, and drizzled with a bit of maple syrup.

Do Ahead The shiitake crumble can be made up to two days in advance and kept in an airtight container at room temperature until ready to serve.

ACTIVE TIME 45 MINUTES
TOTAL TIME 45 MINUTES
MAKES 4 WAFFLES

SWEET QUINOA WAFFLES WITH YOGURT, COCONUT BACON, AND FRUIT COMPOTE

If you can't find quinoa flour, it's easy to make your own if you have a very powerful blender. Just place the quinoa in the blender jar and blitz to a flourlike consistency. Alternatively, you can swap out the quinoa flour for any gluten-free commercial blend. Bob's Red Mill makes a one-for-one blend that works really well in this recipe.

While the "bacon" is roasting, don't walk away from the oven; in the blink of an eye it can go from perfection to a burnt mess. If you're keen to avoid waste, use the leftover egg yolks from the waffle batter in an omelet or custard.

FOR THE COMPOTE

2 small red apples, peeled and cored
¼ cup dried cranberries
1 tablespoon lemon juice
1 tablespoon water

FOR THE WAFFLES

2 cups quinoa flour
2 teaspoons ground cinnamon
Pinch of ground nutmeg
1 tablespoon baking powder
½ teaspoon salt
2 large ripe bananas, peeled and mashed
  (about ¾ cup)
4 large egg whites, lightly beaten
1 tablespoon vanilla extract
2 cups vanilla unsweetened almond milk
Cooking spray

FOR SERVING

1 cup plain yogurt
¼ cup Coconut Bacon (page 127)

1. Make the compote. Combine all the ingredients in a small saucepan. Cover and bring to a simmer over medium-low heat. Cook, stirring occasionally, until the apples are softened, cranberries are plumped, and the compote takes on a syrupy consistency, 5 to 7 minutes. Keep warm while you make the waffles.

2. Make the waffles. Preheat a waffle iron. In a large bowl, whisk together the quinoa flour, cinnamon, nutmeg, baking powder, and salt. Make a well in the center and pour in the bananas, egg whites, vanilla, and almond milk. Stir to combine.

3. Spray the waffle iron with cooking spray and pour in batter. Cook the waffle according to the manufacturer's instructions, until browned and no steam is coming from the sides. Remove and keep warm in a 200°F oven while you cook remaining waffles.

4. To serve, top each waffle with a dollop of yogurt, a sprinkling of coconut bacon, and a spoonful or two of the fruit compote.

Sweet Quinoa Waffle

Brown Rice Waffle

Savory Chickpea Waffle

Tip Many of us have swapped our nonstick cookware for greener and cleaner alternatives that are free of the toxic chemical PFOA. Manufacturers use PFOA to help evenly spread the nonstick coating (such as Teflon) across the pan. The problem? Studies have shown this chemical to linger in the bloodstream, to the point that it's been detected in polar bears and newborn babies. Use of PFOA is now banned, but it could still be in your old-fashioned nonstick waffle maker. If you're in the market for a new waffle iron, check to be sure it's PFOA-free.

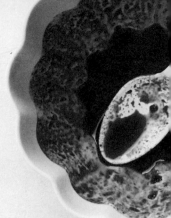

BROWN RICE WAFFLES WITH THREE-BERRY COMPOTE AND COCONUT CREAM

Coconut cream is not to be confused with coconut milk. Coconut cream is only the fat from coconut milk; it makes a great dairy-free whipped cream. Before making the coconut cream, place the bowl of a stand mixer in the fridge to chill; the cold bowl will help the whipped cream stay firm.

FOR THE COMPOTE

2 cups frozen mixed berries, like raspberries, strawberries, and blueberries
3 tablespoons water
¼ cup maple crystals
2 teaspoons fresh lemon juice

FOR THE WAFFLES

1½ cups brown rice flour
¼ cup arrowroot
¼ cup tapioca flour
1 teaspoon xanthan gum
1 tablespoon baking powder
1 teaspoon salt
3 tablespoons turbinado sugar or coconut sugar
1 teaspoon ground cinnamon
2 cups plain unsweetened almond milk
¼ cup coconut oil, melted
Cooking spray

FOR THE COCONUT CREAM

1 (5-ounce) can coconut cream
3 teaspoons grade B organic maple syrup
½ teaspoon vanilla extract

1. Make the compote. In a small saucepan, combine 1 cup of the berries, the water, maple crystals, and lemon juice. Cook over medium heat until the berries begin to break down and a syrup forms, about 10 minutes. Add the remaining cup of berries and cook for another 8 minutes more, stirring frequently. Turn the heat to low to keep the compote warm while you make the waffles.

2. Make the waffles. Preheat a waffle iron. In a large bowl, whisk together the brown rice flour, arrowroot, tapioca flour, xanthan gum, baking powder, salt, sugar, and cinnamon.

3. Make a well in the center and pour in the almond milk and coconut oil. Whisk to combine.

4. Coat the waffle iron with cooking spray and add the batter. Cook the waffle according to the manufacturer's instructions, until browned and no steam is coming from the sides. Remove and keep warm in a 200°F oven while you make the remaining 3 waffles.

5. Make the coconut cream and assemble the dish. In a chilled bowl of a stand mixer, combine the coconut cream, maple syrup, and vanilla. Whip on medium-high speed until light and fluffy, about 1 minute.

6. Top each waffle with a dollop of coconut cream and some berry compote.

Do Ahead The coconut cream can be made up to a week in advance and refrigerated until ready to serve. You'll need to re-whip the cream in a stand mixer until fluffy again.

SUPERCHARGED COFFEE

If you want to kick up your morning cup of Joe, this easy recipe delivers flavor, creaminess, and a nutritional boost. Instead of store-bought coffee creamers full of sugar and artificial flavors, this all-natural version will make any cup good to the last drop.

1 tablespoon grass-fed butter
1 tablespoon coconut oil
8 ounces freshly brewed hot coffee
Optional: chocolate extract, vanilla extract,
  mint extract

Whip together ingredients (with or without one of the extracts) in a blender until homogenous and frothy. Enjoy in place of your morning brew for a sustained winter-worthy warmer.

CHAPTER TWO

simmering soups and stews

Soups and stews are great healthy additions to the *Naturally, Delicious* kitchen recipes that are satisfying and, just as important, filling. The one-pot-meals here run the gamut from vegan and vegetarian recipes, to a meaty Paleo-friendly chicken chili, from gut-healing stocks that make the best use of leftovers to recipes that use healthy and flavorful herbal teas as the base for chilled and piping-hot soups.

Don't be discouraged by the total cooking time required for some of these recipes. A lot of them need a long simmer, which means a slow cooker can come in handy. Load in the ingredients, turn it on, and walk away. *You just need to be patient.* And go ahead and make big batches, even if you're not cooking for a big crew. You can store the leftovers in the refrigerator or freezer and enjoy them later—or improvise by adding leftover chicken, rice, pasta, or beans to give yesterday's pot a whole new look, feel, and taste.

RED HIBISCUS GAZPACHO SOUP

When we were shooting a "mocktails" story in Mexico for the magazine, one of the key ingredients we used to produce a rich, flavorful base for our drinks was fresh hibiscus flowers. These giant, gorgeous red flowers were almost the size of my head. When boiled in water, they produce a dark, floral, fruity tea that makes a really enjoyable sugar-free beverage. In addition to its stunning flavor and color, hibiscus is healthy food, loaded with antioxidants that have been proved to lower blood pressure. Here, I thought the delicious fruity notes of hibiscus could be interesting as a "broth" for gazpacho. And since it can be difficult to source fresh hibiscus flowers, dried will do just fine. You won't be disappointed by this unusual take on the traditional chilled soup. Serve with a dollop of plain Greek yogurt if you like.

4 red hibiscus tea bags

4 cups boiling water

2 (15-ounce) cans whole tomatoes, drained and roughly chopped

1 yellow summer squash, finely diced

1 medium English cucumber, seeded and finely diced

1 red bell pepper, cored, seeded, and finely diced

1 small jalapeño, seeded and minced

3 garlic cloves, minced

1 bunch scallions, white and middle green parts only, sliced

¼ cup olive oil

Juice of 2 limes

1½ tablespoons balsamic vinegar

1½ tablespoons soy sauce

2 teaspoons salt

1 teaspoon ground black pepper

2 tablespoons chopped fresh cilantro

1. Steep the tea bags in the boiling water for 15 minutes. Discard the bags and chill the tea in the refrigerator until cold.

2. In a blender, puree the tomatoes until smooth. Pass through a strainer.

3. In a large bowl or pitcher, combine the remaining ingredients except the yogurt. Stir in the tomato puree and hibiscus tea. Refrigerate until completely chilled, about 2 hours. Taste and season with additional salt and pepper, if needed. Serve cold.

Tip If you have a backyard compost bin, you may think nothing of tossing your old herbal tea bags into it. But you should know that the bag itself is usually not biodegradable, nor are the metal staples and strings. To compost old tea bags, rip open the bags and dump the contents into the compost. Everything else should go into the trash.

GINGER TEA–INFUSED SOUP WITH TOFU, RICE, AND VEGETABLES

Whenever I'm feeling under the weather, I have a home remedy that may not be doctor approved but seems to work like a charm for me. I steep three ginger tea bags in hot water (so far, doctor approved) and add a shot of Jameson whiskey (not approved). It's delicious and literally intoxicating.

Another, more family-friendly use for those ginger tea bags is as a broth substitute. If you love the distinctive flavor of ginger, you'll love this soup. This version is vegetarian, but it would be delicious with shredded leftover chicken and any hearty greens (like kale and chard) you might have on hand.

8 ounces firm tofu

¼ cup tamari

½ cup brown rice, rinsed

1 cup cold water

5 cups boiling water

5 ginger tea bags (I like Yogi Tea brand)

4 garlic cloves, thinly sliced

2 small heads (about 12 ounces) bok choy, trimmed and sliced into ½-inch pieces

2 teaspoons toasted sesame oil

1 bunch scallions, white part only, julienned

1. Place the tofu on a plate and weight down with two more plates; set aside for 30 minutes to press out the liquid. Then drain off the liquid and cut the tofu into 1-inch cubes. Meanwhile, preheat the oven to 425°F.

2. In a small baking dish, toss the tofu with the tamari. Bake until the tofu puffs up and turns golden brown, about 20 minutes, stirring once midway through the baking.

3. In a small pot, combine the rice with the cold water. Cover, bring to a boil, then reduce to a simmer and cook until all the water is absorbed, about 20 minutes. Set aside, covered.

4. In a large pot, combine the boiling water with the ginger tea bags and garlic. Steep for 20 minutes. Discard the tea bags and garlic.

5. Add the tofu and any residual tamari to the pot. Stir in the rice, then add the bok choy and sesame oil. Stir until the bok choy is wilted.

6. Serve the soup garnished with the scallions.

Good to Know Did you know that uncooked white rice has a shelf life of approximately thirty years, but brown rice can be stored in your pantry for only about six months before going bad? The bran in the brown rice (which is stripped away when rice is refined) contains a natural oil that can go rancid. So, buy brown rice in small batches or store it in the refrigerator to extend its shelf life to up to one year.

MATCHA CHICKEN NOODLE SOUP

When it comes to packing a nutritional punch, almost nothing matches matcha, a bright green powder made from the tips of the *Camellia sinensis* tea bush. The fresh leaves go through a complex process of steaming and de-stemming before being ground to a very fine powder. It's an antioxidant powerhouse, provides an energy boost (from a small amount of natural caffeine and other nutrients), supports the immune system, and is even purported to help lower harmful cholesterol. Plus it tastes great. The addition of matcha to a traditional chicken noodle soup makes this the perfect cold and flu season cure-all.

6 cups boiling water

6 teaspoons matcha powder

A 2-inch piece of fresh ginger, cut into ½-inch slices

2 skin-on, bone-in chicken breasts, about 1½ pounds

1 tablespoon salt, or more as needed

2 tablespoons extra-virgin olive oil

1 large onion, diced

4 medium carrots, cut into ½-inch slices

3 celery stalks, cut into ½-inch slices

2 bay leaves

2 cups chicken or vegetable broth

⅓ cup ditalini or other short-cut pasta

Ground black pepper

1. Pour the boiling water into a large bowl. While continually whisking, add the matcha powder 1 teaspoon at a time; the matcha should be fully dissolved. Add the ginger and let cool. Once cooled, discard the ginger slices.

2. Season the chicken all over with 1 teaspoon of the salt.

3. Heat the oil in a large soup pot over medium heat. Add the onion along with 1 teaspoon of the salt. Cover, lower the heat, and cook until softened, about 3 minutes. Add the carrots and celery, and cook, covered, until softened, about 5 minutes, stirring occasionally.

4. Add the bay leaves and chicken, skin side down. Cover and cook for 10 minutes. Flip the chicken, and cook for another 10 minutes. Transfer the chicken to a platter.

5. Add the matcha tea, chicken broth, remaining 1 teaspoon salt, and pepper to taste. Bring to a boil, then lower the heat to a simmer.

6. When the chicken is cool enough to handle, peel off the skin and discard. Pull the meat off the bones (freeze the bones to make Mineral Poultry Bone Broth, page 62, if desired). Cut the chicken into bite-size pieces.

7. Add the chicken and pasta to the pot. Cook until the pasta is cooked through but still chewy, 5 to 6 minutes. Taste and season with additional salt and pepper, if necessary.

Good to Know Once you open a tin of matcha powder, use it as quickly as possible. Matcha is sensitive to light, heat, and air, so it's essential to store it in an airtight container. If you don't plan to finish it within six weeks, store it in the freezer in an airtight, opaque container; you'll double its shelf life.

CHILLED CUCUMBER MINT SOUP

Another tea-infused beauty here. This one's a winner because it utilizes the fresh, bright, palate-cleansing properties of mint in an understated way. It's a bright note in a recipe where the cucumbers and silken tofu take prominence. Some toasted spelt bread with a smear of ricotta cheese turns this soup into dinner.

1 cup water

6 mint tea bags

4 English cucumbers

1 garlic clove, left whole

1 cup silken tofu

1 to 2 tablespoons fresh lemon juice (from 1 lemon)

4 scallions, green and white parts, cut into 1-inch pieces

¼ cup fresh mint leaves, plus 8 large fresh mint leaves sliced into thin ribbons

Salt and freshly ground black pepper

1. In a small pot, bring the water to a boil. Turn the heat off and add the tea bags. Cover and steep for 15 minutes. Remove the tea bags and discard. Cool the tea and refrigerate.

2. Thinly slice half of one cucumber; set aside. Cut the remaining 3½ cucumbers in half lengthwise. Use a spoon to scrape out the seeds from the cucumber halves and discard. Cut 7½ of the cucumber halves into large chunks; cut the remaining piece into small cubes and reserve for the garnish.

3. In a blender, combine the cucumber chunks, the garlic, tofu, 1 tablespoon lemon juice, and chilled mint tea. Puree until smooth. Add the scallions, ¼ cup mint leaves, and salt and pepper to taste. Puree, then taste and season with remaining lemon juice, if desired.

4. Serve the soup garnished with the sliced cucumber and the mint ribbons.

Do Ahead The mint tea can be made ahead and kept in the refrigerator in an airtight container until ready to use.

BONE BROTHS

If New Yorkers see a line, they want in on it. They will queue up to get their hands on the hottest new burger, cupcake, or whatever else is the latest thing a restaurant, food truck, or café is dishing up. But one line definitely worthy of a 30-minute wait is at New York City's Brodo, whose "sipping broths" made from organic ingredients have even the chilliest of New Yorkers warming up to them. Inspired by Brodo, we came up with three types of broth—beef, poultry, and shrimp—which are delicious on their own or as a base for whatever homemade soup you feel like imagining up.

And by the way, bone broth can heal your gut. The digestive tract processes the food we eat, making its nutrients available to the body via the bloodstream. If, however, the tract's lining becomes too porous, nutrients leak out and can cause bloating, cramps, irritable bowel syndrome (IBS), and other problems, including sensitivities to certain foods. Bone broth contains a rich amount of gelatin, which helps reinforce the lining of the gut and soothe digestive distress. So, sip away.

MINERAL POULTRY BONE BROTH

ACTIVE TIME 20 MINUTES
TOTAL TIME 4 HOURS 20 MINUTES
MAKES 6 QUARTS

Chicken soup truly does have medicinal benefits; it's not just an old wives' tale. The soup contains a natural amino acid called cysteine that helps break up and thin the mucus that causes congestion. Recent studies have also shown that store-bought canned or boxed chicken broths do not contain the same levels of cysteine, so Mama's homemade really is best after all. The chicken bones also release nutrient-rich minerals into the broth, including calcium, phosphorus, magnesium, and potassium, which are all easily absorbed into the body as you sip this healthy (and tasty) broth.

You can use any combination of poultry bones including those from a roast turkey or chicken carcass or raw bones and carcass. Collect poultry bones and freeze them until you have enough to make broth; the bones will last up to three months in the freezer.

2 quarts water
2½ pounds organic poultry bones or carcass
1 large onion, quartered
4 medium carrots, cut into thirds
1 celery stalk, cut into thirds
1 small leek, cut into thirds
1 medium sweet potato, quartered
1 bay leaf
½ bunch fresh parsley, coarsely chopped
6 garlic cloves, halved
5 black peppercorns
1 tablespoon apple cider vinegar
1 teaspoon sea salt

1. In a large soup pot, bring the water to a boil. Add the poultry bones, reduce the heat, and simmer for 15 minutes.

2. Add all the remaining ingredients to the pot except the salt, and add enough more water to cover the ingredients by 2 inches. Bring to a boil, then reduce the heat to low, partly cover, and simmer for 4 hours.

3. Strain the broth in batches and discard the solids. Stir in the salt.

Do Ahead Once made, the broth will last one week in the refrigerator or four months in the freezer.

BEEF BONE BROTH

ACTIVE TIME 20 MINUTES
TOTAL TIME 7 HOURS
MAKES 6 QUARTS

If you are using organic vegetables, leave the skins on; if using conventional vegetables, go ahead and peel them. This broth is great on its own or as a rich base for soups, stews, risottos, and sauces. It will keep for about 5 days in the fridge or 4 to 6 months in the freezer.

1½ pounds bones from grass-fed beef
2 tablespoons extra-virgin olive oil
1 large onion, halved
2 large carrots, cut into thirds
6 celery stalks, cut into thirds
1 small leek, cut into thirds
1 parsnip, cut into thirds
1 bay leaf
1 thyme sprig
¼ bunch fresh parsley, chopped
3 garlic cloves, smashed
5 black peppercorns
About 6 quarts water
2 teaspoons salt

1. Preheat the oven to 400°F.

2. Rinse the bones and pat dry. Place them on a parchment-lined baking sheet, drizzle with olive oil, and roast for 40 minutes, turning once halfway.

3. Place the bones in a large stockpot along with the onion, carrots, celery, leek, parsnip, bay leaf, thyme, parsley, garlic, and peppercorns. Add the water, using enough to cover the ingredients by 2 inches. Bring to a boil, then reduce the heat to low. Simmer, partly covered, for 6 hours.

4. Strain the broth and discard the solids. Stir in the salt, and adjust the seasoning.

ACTIVE TIME 10 MINUTES
TOTAL TIME 1 HOUR
MAKES 6 TO 8 CUBES

PHO FLAVOR CUBES

This coconut pho paste is incredibly versatile, but it works deliciously when a few cubes are tossed into Mineral Chicken Broth (page 62). You can also use it as a spread or tossed into hot rice, roasted vegetables, or a seafood salad. Mixing ¼ cup of the pho paste with ¼ cup of the coconut oil aioli makes a delicious dip perfect for crudités or as a mayo replacement for tuna or chicken salad.

5 ounces Thai basil leaves, washed and spun dry

2 ounces mint, washed and spun dry

1 ounce cilantro

4 scallions, trimmed, roughly chopped

2 garlic cloves, minced

3 ounces ginger, minced

1 bird's-eye chili (or other spicy chili)

2 lime leaves (optional)

¼ cup unrefined coconut oil

Sea salt to taste

1. Combine basil, mint, cilantro, scallions, garlic, ginger, chili, lime leaves, and coconut oil in a food processor. Drizzle in oil as machine is running to create a thick puree. Season with salt to taste.

2. Scoop the mixture into ice cube trays and freeze. When the cubes are frozen, pop them out of the tray and store in the freezer in an airtight container until needed.

how to choose
A GREAT COCONUT OIL

It seems like everyone's touting the amazing powers of coconut oil these days. Health experts swear the stuff can help you slim down and boost your brain power. Natural beauty devotees say it's the best skin and hair treatment out there. And vegans love that it can be used instead of butter or lard in baking, since it's solid at room temperature but melts when heated. Personally, I'm a fan of any product that's chemical-free and can be used in lots of ways around the house.

Pick up a jar of coconut oil, and you'll see lots of different buzzwords on the label. But there are really only two things you need to check for: The oil shouldn't be hydrogenated, and it shouldn't be processed using chemicals. Other than that, what you choose is a matter of personal taste.

RAW VS. REFINED
Like the name implies, raw coconut oil is minimally processed. In the nutrition world, "refined" is usually a bad thing, but that's not necessarily the case when it comes to coconut oil. Refined oil has a milder flavor and holds up better to heat, making it a great choice when you're cooking, especially if you don't want a dominant coconuty flavor.

COLD-PRESSED
You might see this on the label, or maybe "expeller-pressed" or "centrifuged." These are all methods of extracting the oil from the coconut flesh that typically don't involve chemicals, and one isn't better than the other. But each produces an oil with a slightly different flavor, so you may need to sample a few to find your favorite.

EXTRA-VIRGIN
If you see this or "virgin" on the label, you can ignore it—in the United States, there's actually no legal definition for these terms when it comes to coconut oil.

15-MINUTE SHRIMP STOCK

As a pescatarian I eat seafood, so I can tell you this stock is lovely on its own, but it also gives a nice flavor boost to gumbo, grits, or rice.

After cleaning the shrimp, save the tails and shells in a plastic bag and freeze them until you have enough to make some stock.

Tails and shells from 3 pounds fresh shrimp
1 small onion, quartered
2 garlic cloves
4 sprigs fresh parsley
5 black peppercorns
1 bay leaf
⅛ teaspoon turmeric
6 cups water

1. Combine all the ingredients in a stockpot, cover, bring to a boil, then lower the heat and simmer for 15 minutes. The stock is done when you can smell the shrimp and the ingredients are softened.

2. Cool the stock and strain and discard the solids. Refrigerate the stock within 2 hours of cooking.

Do Ahead The finished stock will last three to four days in the refrigerator or four to six months in the freezer.

Tip No matter how much he begs, don't give your dog the shrimp tails as a snack, because those barbed tails can get caught in his throat. The sharp edges can also tear the dog's digestive tract, and that would necessitate an emergency room visit.

INDIAN-INSPIRED KAMUT STEW

When we took a trip to India to shoot a "Bucket List Adventure" story for the magazine, I promised my guides I would not venture from the hotel and would not eat street food. Well, that promise was made with my fingers crossed behind my back, because how could I not experience street food, especially as I *love* Indian cuisine?

This recipe reminds me of the stew I got from one of those street vendors, full of traditional Indian ingredients such as earthy red lentils and spices, including hing and nigella seeds—common staples in Indian cooking—layered on a base of root vegetables. The ancient grain Kamut is the healthy twist for this vegetarian wonder.

3 tablespoons coconut oil

1 large onion, coarsely diced

¼ cup minced garlic (from 5 cloves)

¼ cup minced fresh ginger (from 1-ounce root)

1 teaspoon salt

1 teaspoon nigella seeds

1 teaspoon hing

3 curry leaves

1½ pounds celery root, peeled and cut into large dice

1 pound butternut squash, peeled, seeded, and cut into large dice

1 (14-ounce) can tomatoes

1 cup Kamut, soaked overnight and drained

½ cup red lentils

3 cups vegetable stock

¼ cup lime juice (from 1 lime)

Salt and pepper

¼ cup chopped micro greens or fresh cilantro

1. Heat the oil in a large pot. Add the onion, garlic, ginger, and salt, and sauté until onion is translucent, 1 to 2 minutes. Add the nigella seeds, hing, and curry leaves. Sauté 1 minute more.

2. Add the celery root, butternut squash, tomatoes, Kamut, and lentils, and stir to coat with the spices. Sauté for 5 to 10 minutes. Cover the pot, lower the heat, and sweat the vegetables for 10 minutes more, stirring occasionally.

3. Stir in the vegetable stock and bring to a boil. Reduce the heat to low and simmer 45 minutes, or until the stew thickens and the vegetables are very tender. Season with the lime juice and salt and pepper to taste.

4. Garnish with the greens or cilantro and serve.

30-MINUTE TEMPEH CHILI

This has quickly become my go-to meal when I need to serve a crowd at home during chilly weather. I love this fast and furious vegetarian chili because it nevertheless is friendly to people with all sorts of dietary restrictions. No dairy? No problem— just don't add the yogurt. No gluten? This is gluten-free. Love meat? You'll love this more.

Regular tempeh is gluten-free, but varieties called "three-grain tempeh" are not and should be avoided if gluten is on your no-no list. Always read the ingredient label if you're unsure.

¼ cup extra-virgin olive oil, divided

1 (8-ounce) package tempeh, cut into cubes

1 small onion, chopped

2 garlic cloves, minced

1 tablespoon chili powder

2 teaspoons ground cumin

1 teaspoon ground coriander

½ teaspoon salt

1 cup store-bought tomato salsa

1½ cups vegetable broth

1 (15-ounce) can diced fire-roasted tomatoes

1 (15-ounce) can black beans, drained and rinsed

1 tablespoon plain Greek yogurt

1 teaspoon scallions, white and green parts, chopped

1. Warm 3 tablespoons oil in a Dutch oven over medium heat. Add the tempeh and brown on all sides, 5 to 8 minutes, stirring occasionally. Remove from Dutch oven and set aside.

2. Add the remaining tablespoon of oil to the Dutch oven. Add the onion and garlic, cover, and simmer for 5 minutes, stirring often, until the onion starts to soften.

3. Add the chili powder, cumin, coriander, and salt. Cook, stirring, for 1 minute, until well mixed and fragrant. Add the salsa and tempeh to the Dutch oven and stir to coat the tempeh with the spices. Stir in the vegetable broth, tomatoes, and beans. Bring just to a simmer; do not boil. Continue to simmer and stir occasionally until beans are heated through and all ingredients are combined well, 10 to 15 minutes.

4. Garnish the servings of chili with the yogurt and scallions.

Do Ahead You can combine the spices in advance, mix well, and store in a glass jar until needed.

CLASSIC GRASS-FED BEEF CHILI

If you are going to eat meat, it's a good idea to choose organic beef that's from grass-fed cows. Here's why. Traditional factory-style lots feed their cows grain. Great, big silos' worth of grain. Which seems absolutely absurd, when you realize that it's grass that helps cows (and other grazing animals) grow and, in turn, creates more meat. In fact, cows *prefer* grass to grain. Pound for pound, grass-fed is more economical and ecological, and the cows are happier.

2 tablespoons extra-virgin olive oil

1 medium onion, finely diced

3 garlic cloves, minced

1 red bell pepper, cored, seeded, and medium diced

1 pound ground grass-fed beef

2 tablespoons chili powder

1 tablespoon ground cumin

1 teaspoon ground coriander

¼ teaspoon salt

¼ teaspoon cayenne pepper

2 cups beef broth

1 (15-ounce) can diced fire-roasted tomatoes

1 (16-ounce) jar store-bought tomato salsa

1 (15-ounce) can kidney beans, drained and rinsed

1 (15-ounce) can pinto beans, drained and rinsed

¼ cup shredded Cheddar cheese

2 scallions, white and green parts, chopped

1 tablespoon chopped fresh cilantro

Tortilla chips

1. Heat the oil in a large Dutch oven over medium heat. Add the onion, garlic, and red pepper. Cover and cook for 5 minutes, stirring occasionally, until the onion is translucent.

2. Add the ground beef. Using a wooden spoon, break up the beef, cover the pot, and cook for 5 minutes, until the beef is browned.

3. Stir in the chili powder, cumin, coriander, salt, and cayenne; cook for 1 minute. Stir in the beef broth, tomatoes, and salsa. Bring to a simmer, then add the beans. Cover and simmer for 20 minutes.

4. Serve the chili garnished with the cheese, scallions, and cilantro. Accompany with tortilla chips.

Tip Since there are no strict standards for "grass-fed" beef in the United States, the next best thing is to look for a mark on the package from a third-party operation. The best mark is from the American Grassfed Association, which most sustainability experts agree has the best definition, procedures, and certification methods for ensuring you're getting real grass-fed meat products.

SHAKE-AND-BAKE
MEDITERRANEAN BEEF STEW

For some reason, I was obsessed with the product Shake 'n Bake as a child. It seemed so simple: throw the chicken pieces into the bag, shake with the seasoned bread crumbs, and bake. Dinner! Maybe it was the commercials? Maybe it was the ease of it all? But I do know my mother never shook or baked a thing.

This recipe isn't exactly an homage to the family classic; it's more of a healthy gourmet rendition. If you don't want to mess up a roasting bag, you can also mix it all up in a bowl. But where's the nostalgic fun in that?

FOR THE SPICE MIX

1 tablespoon ground cumin
1 tablespoon ground coriander
1 tablespoon salt
1½ teaspoons ground rosemary
1½ teaspoons ground thyme
1½ teaspoons ground sage
1 teaspoon ground black pepper

FOR THE STEW

1½ pounds boneless beef for stew
2 tablespoons extra-virgin olive oil
1 medium onion, diced
2 garlic cloves, minced
4 carrots, cut into ½-inch slices
2 celery stalks, cut into ½-inch slices
½ cup dry red wine
5 cups beef or vegetable broth
1 cup plus 3 tablespoons water
2 bay leaves
About 2 teaspoons salt
1 teaspoon ground black pepper
1 tablespoon arrowroot
3 russet potatoes, peeled and cut into eighths
¼ cup fresh parsley, chopped

1. Make the spice mixture. Combine the spice ingredients in a small bowl.

2. Make the stew. In a large brown paper bag, combine the meat with ¼ cup of the spice mix. Shake until the meat is evenly coated.

3. In a 5-quart pot, heat the olive oil over high heat. Working in batches, brown the seasoned meat on all sides, about 3 to 4 minutes. Using a slotted spoon, transfer the browned meat to a plate.

4. Add the onion and garlic to the pot, cover, and cook until softened, about 3 minutes. Add the carrots and celery; cover and cook until softened, about 5 minutes.

5. Add the wine. Using a wooden spoon, scrape the pot to loosen any solids on the bottom. Add the broth, 1 cup water, bay leaves, 1 teaspoon salt, and the pepper.

6. In a small bowl, dissolve the arrowroot in the remaining 3 tablespoons water. Stir into the stew. Add the potatoes and cover the pot. Simmer the stew over low heat for 1 hour.

7. When the meat is tender and the potatoes are soft, the stew is ready. Taste and season with additional salt, if needed. Serve garnished with the chopped parsley.

Tip Reuse glass jars that once held jams and jellies to store your dried spices. Just run the jars and lids in the dishwasher so they are thoroughly cleaned and sanitized, and allow them to fully dry. Then, fill the jars with your own dried herbs or the herbs from the bulk bins at the market, thereby avoiding the more expensive small jars of herbs at the supermarket.

PALEO CHICKEN CHILI

I once dated someone who went on a Paleo diet; my friend eventually became so obsessed with eating like a caveman that everything I ate was pronounced "toxic" and "poison." Needless to say, that relationship didn't last very long.

Even though my little interaction with the world of Paleo eating was short-lived, what I do know is this: a lot of people are eating this way. So, I challenged our recipe partners at the Natural Gourmet Institute to come up with a Paleo-friendly chili that was not just good but also the greatest chicken chili *ever*. Mission accomplished.

2 tablespoons extra-virgin olive oil
1 medium onion, diced (about 1 cup)
2 tablespoons ground cumin
2 tablespoons chili powder
2 teaspoons garlic powder
½ teaspoon ground coriander
½ teaspoon dried oregano
½ teaspoon chipotle seasoning
¼ teaspoon red pepper flakes
3 small carrots, diced (about 1 cup)
3 celery stalks, chopped (about 1 cup)
1 red bell pepper, cored, seeded, and diced
1 teaspoon salt
¼ teaspoon ground black pepper
1 pound ground chicken
2 cups low-sodium chicken stock
3 scallions, shredded lengthwise
2 tablespoons fresh cilantro leaves

1. In a 4-quart pot, heat the olive oil over medium-low heat. Add the onion and cook until slightly softened, about 2 minutes.

2. Add the cumin, chili powder, garlic powder, coriander, oregano, chipotle seasoning, and red pepper flakes. Cook until fragrant, about 1 minute, stirring often.

3. Add the carrots, celery, red pepper, salt, and black pepper. Cook until the vegetables are softened, about 10 minutes.

4. Add the chicken and cook until browned, using a wooden spoon to break up the chicken, about 10 minutes.

5. Add the chicken stock and bring to a boil. Cover the pot, lower the heat, and simmer for 1 hour. Uncover the pot and cook until the liquid is somewhat reduced, about 20 more minutes.

6. Served the chili garnished with scallions and cilantro.

Tip Every year, restaurants and commercial kitchens throw out tons of food that is considered excess inventory and that could otherwise be given to food banks. One of the problems of getting the excess food to the charities is often there isn't enough manpower to pick up and bring the food to the shelter. Contact your local food bank and ask if they need any volunteer "food runners." It's one easy step to help stop waste and alleviate hunger.

"eat,
sleep,
snack,
repeat."

a little in-between snacking

I meet a lot of really healthy people in my line of work: dietitians, nutritionists, and personal trainers. I love chatting with them because they make me reexamine some of my so-called good habits. For instance, one time I proudly told a nutritionist how much water I was drinking each day, and she warned me that "I could drown." So much for that good intention.

But turnabout is fair play. When these healthy, perfect specimens are done sharing their wisdom with our readers, I usually have one last question for them: "You're in a 7-Eleven and you have to eat something. What's it going to be?" Sometimes the answer is boxed macaroni and cheese made from the bright, nuclear-orange powder. Often, it's the simple potato chip (which is actually minimally processed but still deep fried and addictively delicious). And once in a while, someone confesses to the ultimate guilty pleasures: Ho Hos, Twinkies, or Pepperidge Farm cookies.

The point is this: we all love to snack. Sometimes (I'm thinking something in nugget form you dip and repeat), the simplicity of snacking can even replace a meal. You're not starving, but you're in the mood to nosh. It's like ordering off the kid's menu and having a glass of wine. The portions and combination are *just right*.

What I've done here is taken familiar childhood favorites and time-warped them to the future. We've swapped out unhealthy for the healthy, but kept the crispy, ooey-gooey, crunchy textures we all love.

BROWN-BAG POPCORN FOUR WAYS

Let me be blunt: microwave popcorn is gross. Don't believe me? Go ahead and open one before you pop it. That gelatinous mess of kernels, fats, and other unrecognizable solids melts down, heats up, and becomes a bowl of hot popcorn. Even worse, the nonstick bag is lined with the same chemicals as used to make the nonstick frying pans that are being phased out.

If you like the convenience of microwave popcorn but not the death scare, give these a try. Regular brown paper bags work great, and you won't have to worry about what evils lurk inside your popcorn bag.

FOR ALL: ACTIVE TIME 5 MINUTES
TOTAL TIME 20 MINUTES
SERVES 4

BROWN-BAG POPCORN

¼ cup popcorn kernels
1 lunch-size brown paper bag

1. Make the popcorn. Place the kernels in the brown paper bag and fold down the top two or three times to close.

2. Microwave on high until the popping slows down, about 4 minutes.

TRUFFLE-PARMESAN POPCORN

Brown-Bag Popcorn
⅔ cup freshly grated Parmesan cheese
½ teaspoon truffle oil
2 tablespoons chopped fresh parsley
Salt

While the popcorn is still hot, sprinkle the cheese, truffle oil, parsley, and salt to taste into the brown bag. Reseal the bag, shake to combine, and serve.

CHIPOTLE-MAPLE POPCORN

Brown-Bag Popcorn
½ cup grade B organic maple syrup
2 tablespoons extra-virgin olive oil
1 teaspoon chipotle seasoning
½ teaspoon salt

1. Preheat the oven to 300°F. Pour the prepared popcorn onto a parchment-lined baking sheet.

2. In a small saucepan, combine the maple syrup, olive oil, chipotle seasoning, and salt. Bring to a boil over medium heat, stirring just until combined.

3. Drizzle the syrup evenly over the popcorn. Toss with a rubber spatula to coat thoroughly.

4. Bake for 15 minutes. Cool completely before serving.

PEANUT-BANANA POPCORN

Brown-Bag Popcorn
½ cup honey
¼ cup grade B organic maple syrup
½ cup raw peanut butter
½ teaspoon vanilla extract
½ teaspoon salt
½ cup dried banana chips
¼ cup fair-trade dark chocolate chips

1. Preheat the oven to 300°F. Place the prepared popcorn on a parchment-lined baking sheet.

2. In a small saucepan, combine the honey, maple syrup, peanut butter, vanilla, and salt. Stir over medium heat until smooth.

3. Drizzle the syrup evenly over the popcorn and sprinkle with the banana chips and chocolate chips. Toss with a rubber spatula to coat thoroughly.

4. Bake for 10 minutes. Cool completely before serving.

CRISPY PARMESAN CAULIFLOWER TOTS

For several years I ate a strict vegan diet, and during that period I also tried a low-carb diet for a day. What I discovered is that once you eliminate the basic carbohydrate staples of a vegan diet (pasta, rice, bread, and fruit), you are pretty much just left with vegetables and olive oil. And water.

On that one Atkins-celebratory day, I lived on cauliflower mash. After two servings, the mash was losing its appeal, so I decided to mold it into "tots," which I rolled in bread crumbs for a nice crunch. A little drizzle of olive oil and I baked them to golden perfection. Fifteen years later, I haven't forgotten that awful carb-less day, but at least these tots have earned a permanent place on my crunchy crispy snack roster.

1 tablespoon olive oil, for the baking sheet
1 pound organic frozen cauliflower florets
½ cup gluten-free bread crumbs
¼ cup grated Parmesan cheese
1 large egg
2 tablespoons chopped fresh parsley
¼ teaspoon garlic powder
¼ teaspoon black pepper

1. Preheat the oven to 400°F. Line a baking sheet with parchment paper and brush with olive oil.

2. Microwave the cauliflower according to the package directions, and cool to room temperature.

3. Place the cauliflower on a clean dish towel or piece of cheesecloth, and roll it up and wring it out to extract as much moisture from the cauliflower as you can. Transfer the cauliflower to a large bowl and break apart the florets with your hands. Add the bread crumbs, cheese, egg, parsley, garlic powder, and pepper. Using your hands, mix until the mixture holds together.

4. Using a tablespoon measure, scoop the cauliflower onto the prepared baking sheet. Use your hands to roll each scoop into an oval-shaped tot.

5. Bake for 15 minutes, remove from the oven, turn the tots over, and bake for another 15 minutes to crisp the other side. Serve warm.

ACTIVE TIME 20 MINUTES
TOTAL TIME 1 HOUR 5 MINUTES
MAKES 20 CROQUETTES AND ½ CUP AÏOLI

BAKED SWEET POTATO CROQUETTES

True story: a fellow magazine editor at *Men's Health* recently mentioned that before a cover shoot, their male models eat sweet potatoes for days. He claimed they help draw water out of the body to reduce bloating and make those washboard abs look even more chiseled.

I love sweet potatoes, so I made this croquette recipe a few times that week, and though they were delicious, I did not notice a single change in my appearance. When I complained to my friend, he explained that I hadn't listened carefully. Apparently these six-pack–bearing models eat nothing *but* baked sweet potatoes—and completely unadorned.

This version tastes a lot better than a plain baked sweet potato and it beats any conventional croquette. We bake rather than fry 'em and use only whole ingredients. Just go easy on the mayo sauce if you have a shirtless cover shoot coming up.

1 pound sweet potatoes, peeled and cut into
 1-inch cubes
1 tablespoon extra-virgin olive oil
1 large egg, lightly beaten
½ cup fresh goat cheese
½ cup grated Parmesan cheese
½ teaspoon salt
Pinch of black pepper
2 tablespoons chopped fresh parsley
2 to 2½ cups gluten-free bread crumbs
Chive Aïoli or Vegan Coconut Aïoli

1. Make the croquettes. Place the sweet potatoes in a medium pot with cold water to cover by about 2 inches. Cover the pot and bring to a boil. Reduce the heat to low, place the lid askew, and simmer until the potatoes can easily be pierced with a fork, about 15 minutes. Drain, return the potatoes to the pot, and let cool.

2. Preheat the oven to 400°F. Line a baking sheet with parchment paper and grease with olive oil.

3. In a large bowl, use a fork to mash together the sweet potatoes, the egg, goat cheese, Parmesan, salt, pepper, parsley, and ¾ cup bread crumbs. The mixture should be a little sticky but firm enough to hold together; mix in more bread crumbs, if needed.

4. Place 1 cup breadcrumbs in a shallow dish.

5. Scoop out tablespoon-size croquettes and form into patties with your hands. Dredge both sides of the croquettes in the bread crumbs and place on the prepared baking sheet.

6. Bake the croquettes for 15 minutes; flip and cook for another 15 minutes.

7. Serve hot with the aïoli of your choice.

ACTIVE TIME 5 MINUTES
TOTAL TIME 5 MINUTES
MAKES 1 CUP

CHIVE AÏOLI

If making aïoli, essentially a homemade mayonnaise, intimidates you, go ahead and use store-bought mayo as the base. That said, I promise this is easy and tastes a whole lot better, too.

1 large egg yolk

2 garlic cloves, minced

1 tablespoon fresh lemon juice, or more to taste

¼ teaspoon salt, or more to taste

¼ cup canola oil

¼ cup extra-virgin olive oil

2 tablespoons chopped fresh chives

1. In a small bowl, whisk together the egg yolk, garlic, lemon juice, and salt.

2. While whisking continually, slowly stream in the canola oil, followed by the olive oil. Stir in the chives. Taste and season with a bit more salt or lemon juice, if needed.

Do Ahead The aïoli can be made one day ahead and refrigerated in an airtight container.

Good to Know To make the aïoli using store-bought mayo, whisk together ⅔ cup mayo, 1 tablespoon lemon juice, 1 teaspoon Dijon mustard, 2 tablespoons chopped chives, and 1 minced garlic clove until smooth.

VEGAN COCONUT AÏOLI

This sauce's delicate coconut flavor has a myriad of uses, but it's my go-to mayonnaise alternative for sandwiches. Some toasted gluten-free bread, a little of this aïoli, and whatever I can find in the fridge makes for one great late-night snack.

4 ounces soft silken tofu

2 teaspoons fresh lemon juice

1 teaspoon Dijon mustard

¾ cup organic non-GMO canola oil

¼ cup coconut oil

Sea salt

1. Combine the tofu, lemon juice, and mustard in a blender and puree for about 30 seconds or until the tofu is smooth.

2. While blending, slowly add in the oils until the mixture thickens.

3. Season to taste with sea salt.

TROPICAL GUACAMOLE WITH SPIRULINA

"Spiru-what now?" you may be asking yourself. Spirulina is a blue-green algae, usually sold in powder form, that really first took off (no pun intended) when astronauts in space used it as a dietary supplement. It's easy to understand why it's NASA-approved: spirulina is rich in protein, vitamin B_{12}, and iron. It's also rich in chlorophyll, which is believed to help remove toxins from the body.

Many *really* healthy people like to drink spirulina straight up, in warm water. My advice? Don't. The taste can be off-putting, like—well—warm pond water. But a small amount mixed into your guacamole is virtually undetectable and gives your chips and dip a big healthy boost. Look for it in natural food stores.

4 Hass avocados, peeled, pitted, and chopped

1 cup finely diced pineapple

1 mango, peeled, pitted, and diced (½ cup)

½ small red onion, finely diced

1 jalapeño, seeded and minced

¼ cup fresh lime juice (from 4 limes), or more to taste

1 tablespoon chopped fresh cilantro

1 tablespoon spirulina powder, plus more for garnish

½ teaspoon salt, or more to taste

1. Mash the avocados in a large bowl. Stir in the pineapple, mango, red onion, jalapeño, lime juice, cilantro, spirulina, and ½ teaspoon salt.

2. Transfer the guacamole to a serving dish. Taste and season with additional salt and lime juice, if needed. Just before serving, sprinkle with a bit of additional spirulina.

Do Ahead The guacamole can be prepared two hours ahead and refrigerated until ready to serve.

Tip It's not easy to buy everything organic, but in reality it's not always necessary. Avocados, for instance, have a thick skin that makes the likelihood of any pesticides leaching through to the flesh very remote.

ZA'ATAR CACIK DIP WITH CRUDITÉS

It's tempting to go to the supermarket and pick up a few tubs of pre-made dip and washed-and-cut veggies and arrange that on a platter for your next party. But when you realize how easy it is to make a really good dip that's fresh, you'll never go back to those tubs.

1 small English cucumber

8 ounces plain Greek yogurt

2 garlic cloves, minced

1 teaspoon za'atar

2 tablespoons minced fresh mint

Julienne slices of zucchini, yellow squash, bell pepper, broccoli, carrots

2 teaspoons extra-virgin olive oil

1. Halve and seed the cucumber, then grate. Place in a colander and drain well.

2. In a medium bowl, stir together the drained cucumber, the yogurt, garlic, za'atar, and 1 tablespoon of the mint. Transfer to a serving bowl and arrange the vegetables around it.

3. To serve, drizzle the dip with the oil and sprinkle with the remaining 1 tablespoon mint.

CLASSIC HUMMUS

Seriously, don't ever buy store-bought hummus ever, ever, ever again! Once you try this, you'll be hooked on homemade. And you can use this classic hummus base to be creative. For instance, I add a dollop of miso at the end to give it an Asian flavor—a wink and a nod to my heritage.

1 (15-ounce) can chickpeas, with liquid

2 to 3 garlic cloves, minced

¾ cup tahini

½ teaspoon sea salt

1 to 2 tablespoons fresh lemon juice, or more to taste

3 tablespoons plus 2 teaspoons extra-virgin olive oil

1 teaspoon za'atar or smoked paprika

1. In a food processor, combine the chickpeas and their liquid, with the garlic, tahini, salt, and 1 tablespoon of the lemon juice. With the motor running, stream in 3 tablespoons of the olive oil. Puree until smooth and creamy, scraping down once or twice as needed. Taste and season with more salt or lemon juice, if needed.

2. Transfer the mixture to a serving bowl and drizzle with the remaining 2 teaspoons olive oil. Sprinkle with za'atar.

Do Ahead The hummus can be refrigerated in an airtight container for up to one week. Bring to room temperature before serving.

ACTIVE TIME 10 MINUTES
TOTAL TIME 20 MINUTES
MAKES 2 CUPS
SERVES 4

SWEET POTATO HUMMUS

I once saw an advertisement for a national hummus brand that had the tagline "We put the chic in chickpeas." Clever. This recipe is more than just a rebranding, though; it gets a radical twist with the addition of sweet potatoes.

This dip is addictive and so good for you: heart healthy and loaded with vitamins A, C, and almost all the Bs, plus potassium, fiber, niacin, and copper. Spread it on toast or just grab a bag of organic blue corn tortilla chips and snack away.

If you do not own a food processor, you can easily mash and combine the ingredients with a fork, then beat with a whisk to achieve a smooth texture.

3 medium sweet potatoes, halved lengthwise

1 tablespoon coconut oil

⅓ cup tahini

¼ cup fresh lime juice (from 6 limes)

3 garlic cloves, minced

1½ teaspoons ground cumin

⅛ teaspoon ground turmeric

½ teaspoon salt

½ teaspoon ground black pepper, plus more for garnish

1 teaspoon extra-virgin olive oil

1. Rub the sweet potato halves with the coconut oil on all sides, including the skin. Pierce the skin with a fork in several places. Microwave on high until a fork can easily pierce the flesh and the skin feels soft to the touch, 3 to 4 minutes. When they are cool enough to handle, peel off the skin and discard.

2. Place the sweet potatoes in a shallow dish and mash with a fork. Allow to come to room temperature.

3. In a food processor, combine the sweet potatoes, tahini, lime juice, garlic, cumin, turmeric, salt, and pepper. Puree until smooth. Taste and adjust the seasonings, if necessary.

4. To serve, drizzle with the olive oil and sprinkle with the black pepper.

CILANTRO-EDAMAME HUMMUS

Cilantro is one of those herbs that's like the Kardashians: you either *really really* love it or you *really really* hate it. If you belong to the latter camp, you can swap out cilantro for flat-leaf parsley or mint.

This can also be mashed up with a fork if you don't have a food processor. And if you really dislike the flavor of cilantro, you can omit it to make a just-as-nice edamame hummus.

¾ cup frozen shelled edamame

2 garlic cloves, chopped

¼ cup tahini

½ cup water

¼ cup packed fresh cilantro leaves

¼ teaspoon ground cumin

Pinch of cayenne pepper, plus more
  for garnish

2 tablespoons extra-virgin olive oil

½ teaspoon salt

1 to 2 tablespoons lemon juice (from
  1 lemon), or more to taste

1 tablespoon chopped cilantro, for garnish

1. Place the edamame in a microwave-safe bowl and microwave on high until soft, about 2½ minutes. Set aside to cool.

2. In a food processor, combine the edamame, garlic, tahini, water, cilantro leaves, cumin, cayenne, olive oil, salt, and 1 tablespoon lemon juice. Puree until smooth, scraping down the sides of the bowl once or twice as needed. Taste and season with a bit more salt and lemon juice, if needed.

3. Serve garnished with chopped cilantro and a bit of cayenne.

Sweet Potato Hummus

Cilantro-Edamame Hummus

APRICOT PECAN POWER BARS

In a perfect world, you'd refuel with one of these power bars after going vertically up a mountainside for several miles. In reality, you might be camped outside a department store waiting for the Black Friday bargains to begin. Whichever scenario you're more likely to find yourself in, these are a pretty good source of energy that are also really easy to make. I think they are just as good without chocolate, but a roomful of chocoholics begged to differ. You can decide for yourself.

1 cup dried apricots

2 cups raw pecans

2 large eggs

¼ teaspoon salt

3 tablespoons chia seeds

1 tablespoon vanilla extract

1 cup fair-trade dark chocolate chips

1. Preheat the oven to 350°F. Line an 8-inch square baking pan with parchment paper.

2. In a food processor, pulse the apricots and pecans until ground to pea-size bits. Add the eggs, salt, chia seeds, and vanilla, and pulse until a ball forms. Transfer the mixture to a bowl and stir in ½ cup of the chocolate chips with a wooden spoon.

3. Press the mixture evenly into the prepared baking dish and sprinkle with the remaining ½ cup of chocolate chips. Bake for 25 minutes.

4. Let cool before cutting into bars and serving.

Do Ahead These power bars can be prepared one week in advance, cut into bars, and individually wrapped, and stored in the fridge until you're ready to grab and go.

"HALVA" BARS WITH SORGHUM

One of the best Paleo-style ancient—or heritage—grains is sorghum, which was discovered 8,000 years ago growing in southern Egypt. Unlike genetically modified wheat, sorghum has remained pretty much the same today as it was back then. And that means it's tolerable for all of us: it's gluten-free and nutritious too, because it's high in iron and fiber.

These bars use sorghum in an unusual way: we pop the grains. It makes them airy and delicious. Think of this as our healthier version of halva—a traditional Middle Eastern confection—made with slightly sweet sorghum, popped like popcorn. (This technique works with millet and amaranth, too.)

2 cups sorghum

2 cups rolled oats

1 teaspoon salt

2 teaspoons sumac

½ cup sesame seeds

1 teaspoon dried thyme

⅔ cup tahini

¾ cup grade B organic maple syrup

1. Heat a heavy pot with a tight-fitting lid over medium-high heat. Add ¼ cup of the sorghum at a time and cover the pot. When the sorghum grains begin to pop (you will hear it), shake the pot until the popping stops, 2 to 3 minutes. Most, but not all, of the grains will pop. Transfer the popped grain to a bowl and pop the remaining sorghum, cooking it ¼ cup at a time. Pick through the popped sorghum and remove any unpopped grains after each batch.

2. Preheat the oven to 350°F. Oil a 9 by 13-inch baking pan and line it with parchment paper.

3. Measure 2 cups of popped sorghum into a large mixing bowl. Add the oats, salt, sumac, sesame seeds, and thyme, and mix well.

4. In a small bowl, whisk together the tahini and maple syrup. Pour the tahini-maple mixture into the popped sorghum mixture. Stir with a spatula until well mixed.

5. Press the mixture into the prepared pan. Bake 25 minutes, or until golden at the edges. Place the pan on a wire rack to cool completely. When cool, invert the pan onto a cutting board and cut into 16 bars.

Tip If you plan on wrapping these bars in wax paper, choose the unbleached kind. Conventional wax paper is coated in paraffin, which is a wax made from petroleum. When you use unbleached wax paper, the bars will be in contact with a food-grade wax—usually soybean wax—that's clean, nontoxic, and a renewable resource.

HONEY-SPELT LOAF

I'm sure you can tell by now that I am a fan of kitchen shortcuts. If you've got one of those handy-dandy breadmakers at home, this will work beautifully in it. Just dump in all the ingredients and push a button. But if not, it's still easy enough to make this bread conventionally.

The optimal temperature for warm water in this recipe is 105°F, so use a candy thermometer if you've got one.

Canola oil or sunflower oil

1¾ cups warm (105°F) water

1 tablespoon plus 1 teaspoon raw honey

3 teaspoons active dry yeast

3 cups spelt flour

½ tablespoon sea salt

½ cup flax, sesame, and/or sunflower seeds

1. Lightly grease a 9 by 5-inch loaf pan with canola or sunflower oil.

2. In a measuring cup or small bowl, combine the water, honey, and yeast. Set aside for a few minutes, until bubbles begin to form.

3. In a large mixing bowl, combine the flour, salt, and ¼ cup of the seeds. Add the yeast mixture and stir until a thick and moist dough is formed.

4. Pour into the prepared loaf pan and smooth the top. Sprinkle with the remaining ¼ cup of the seeds. Cover with a greased piece of plastic wrap and place a tea towel on top. Place the bowl on the top of the stove where it is warm, and let it rise for 20 to 30 minutes, until it has almost doubled in size. Meanwhile, preheat the oven to 375°F.

5. Bake the loaf for 40 minutes, or until a tester inserted in the center comes out clean. Remove from the pan and let cool on a wire rack before slicing.

Tip Some projects to feed wild birds during the winter months involve coating a piece of bread with peanut butter and bird seed and hanging it from a tree. Bird experts agree this practice should be avoided because the bread offers few nutrients to birds, who need fat to survive, not carbohydrates. A better option is to coat a pinecone with natural peanut butter and roll that in birdseed.

CHAPTER FOUR

lovely lunches

Maybe it's a result of living in nonstop New York City for fifteen years, but when 12:30 P.M. comes around, I'm usually chained to my desk at the magazine's New York City offices. My grumbling stomach isn't a signal that I'll soon be enjoying a three-course meal al fresco; it's just a routine reminder to not forget to eat.

My typical lunch is a massaged kale salad with white cannellini beans or chickpeas tossed with a simple vinaigrette. I make it at home and pack it in a metal tiffin; top layer has the salad and the bottom compartment a piece of fruit. As one hand types away on my laptop, the other hand feeds my mouth. Kale. Chew. Edit. Repeat.

But when I do have time to slow down at home, it's nice to embrace a more European sensibility and make something from scratch—either to eat then or pack along to the office. What I love about these lunch ideas is that if you invest the time to make homemade tortillas, wraps, or whole-grain salads you can enjoy some of it for lunch and save the rest to make something entirely different for dinner. Suddenly, supper becomes fast food, minus the greasy takeout or pizza delivery.

And if you're like me and need a little something sweet to finish off your lunch, try a piece of perfectly ripe fruit or make a big batch of *Naturally, Delicious* bars, cookies, or other packable treats. The Italians are famous for embracing *dolce far Niente* (the sweetness of doing nothing), but even on my most hectic day, I can find a spare minute to at least enjoy the dolce as I edit pages of the magazine and nibble a cookie.

FRIED CHICKEN LIVER SANDWICHES WITH PICKLED RED ONION AND ARUGULA

When Dan Akroyd famously played Julia Child on *Saturday Night Live*, perhaps his most memorable line was "Save the liver!" Joking aside, he (or she?) had a point: the liver can be delicious.

With some 40 percent of all perfectly good food thrown away in the United States every year, there's a growing movement to use as much of an animal as possible when it comes to butchery. An easy way to see past perfect cutlets and drumsticks is to buy the chicken livers for recipes like this tasty sandwich.

FOR THE PICKLED RED ONIONS

½ cup apple cider vinegar
1 cup maple, coconut, or turbinado sugar
1½ teaspoons salt
1 medium red onion, thinly sliced

FOR THE CHICKEN LIVERS

¼ cup buttermilk
Sea salt
Freshly ground black pepper
1 pound chicken livers, trimmed
  (about 8 livers)
½ cup all-purpose flour
½ cup whole wheat flour
½ teaspoon onion powder
½ teaspoon garlic powder
¼ teaspoon smoked paprika
¼ teaspoon cayenne pepper
3 tablespoons canola oil

FOR ASSEMBLING THE SANDWICHES

4 tablespoons mayonnaise
1 whole wheat baguette, split lengthwise
2 cups baby arugula

1. Make the pickled onions. In a small bowl, whisk together the vinegar, sugar, and salt. Add the onion and stir to combine. Cover tightly with plastic wrap and let sit at room temperature for 1 hour.

2. Make the livers. In a large bowl, whisk together the buttermilk, ½ teaspoon salt, and ¼ teaspoon pepper. Add the chicken livers and toss to coat. Cover with plastic wrap and refrigerate for 15 minutes.

3. Meanwhile, in a shallow dish, whisk together the flours, onion powder, garlic powder, paprika, cayenne, and a couple of pinches of the salt and pepper.

4. Drain the chicken livers and discard the marinade. Dredge the livers in the flour mixture and shake off excess flour.

5. In a large cast-iron skillet, heat the oil over medium-high heat. When the oil starts to shimmer, fry the chicken livers in a single layer until golden and crisp, 8 to 10 minutes, turning once halfway. Transfer the livers to a paper towel–lined plate.

6. Assemble the sandwiches. Spread the mayonnaise on both sides of the baguette. Place the chicken livers on the bottom half and top with the pickled onions and arugula. Close the baguette and cut into 4 portions.

Do Ahead The pickled onions can be made up to two weeks ahead and kept in the fridge until ready to serve.

CASSAVA-SPINACH TORTILLAS WITH SHREDDED CHICKEN, HUMMUS, AND VEGGIES

"Cassava" sounds like the title of a Telemundo soap opera, but it's actually tapioca flour. It may seem like overkill to make your own tortillas from scratch, but it's worth it. You can fill them with whatever you have on hand in the fridge, and you can make the filled tortillas sweet or savory, meaty or vegetarian, and even vegan.

FOR THE TORTILLAS

4 cups packed baby spinach

¼ cup water

2 tablespoons extra-virgin olive oil

1 cup cassava flour (tapioca flour)

½ teaspoon sea salt

FOR THE CHICKEN AND VEGETABLES

2 tablespoons extra-virgin olive oil

3 garlic cloves, minced

2 boneless, skinless chicken breasts, sliced into thin strips

½ teaspoon sea salt

¼ teaspoon freshly ground black pepper

8 ounces cremini mushrooms, stemmed and sliced

1 red bell pepper, cored, seeded, and thinly sliced

2 to 3 tablespoons low-sodium soy sauce

1 tablespoon brown rice vinegar

1 tablespoon mirin

1 pint cherry tomatoes, halved

4 ounces prepared hummus

1. Make the tortillas. Over medium heat, combine the spinach and water in a large pan. Cover and bring to a simmer. Cook until spinach wilts, 2 to 3 minutes. Transfer the spinach and cooking liquid to a food processor. Add the oil and puree until smooth. Let cool.

2. In a large bowl, whisk together the cassava flour and salt. Using a wooden spoon, stir in the cooled spinach mixture. If the mixture appears too dry and crumbly, sprinkle in 1 tablespoon water. Continue mixing by hand until the dough is smooth and soft. If dough is still sticking to your hands, sprinkle in a bit of water and continue kneading.

3. Divide the dough into 6 lumps and roll into balls. Place on a platter, cover with a damp paper towel, and refrigerate for 30 minutes.

4. Heat a nonstick pan over low heat. Place a ball of dough between two pieces of parchment paper and roll out to a 6-inch diameter. Place in the hot skillet and cook the tortilla until it starts to brown in places, 3 to 4 minutes. Flip and cook for another 3 to 4 minutes. Remove and continue making remaining tortillas.

5. Make the chicken and vegetables. Heat 1 tablespoon of the oil in a large nonstick pan over medium heat. Add the garlic and cook until fragrant, about 1 minute. Add the chicken, season with salt and pepper, and cook until browned, 5 to 7 minutes. Transfer to a plate.

6. Add the remaining tablespoon oil to the skillet and stir in the mushrooms and bell pepper. Cook until the vegetables start to brown, about 2 minutes. Stir in the soy sauce, vinegar, and mirin, and then add the tomatoes. Cook for 1 minute. Return the chicken to the skillet and toss with the vegetables until warmed through.

7. To serve, spread some of the hummus on each tortilla and top with the chicken and vegetables.

ACTIVE TIME 35 MINUTES
TOTAL TIME 40 MINUTES
MAKES 9 TORTILLAS

QUINOA TORTILLAS WITH TROPICAL FRUIT AND TAHINI

Quinoa tortillas are not hard to make and have a thousand uses. This quick, fruity filling works well for breakfast, too. For the tortilla recipe, you will need water that is hot but not boiling. When shaping the tortillas, roll from the center out, turning the paper slightly after each roll. Continue turning and rolling until you've made a flat, circular tortilla. Brown parchment paper is easier and more flexible with this dough.

FOR THE QUINOA TORTILLAS

2 cups quinoa flour
¼ cup plus 2 tablespoons brown rice flour
1 teaspoon salt
1½ teaspoons olive oil
¾ cup hot water

FOR THE FILLING

¼ cup coconut flakes
⅓ cup tahini
4 teaspoons honey
2 teaspoons fresh lime juice (from 1 lime)
1 mango, peeled, pitted, and diced
8 small Medjool dates, pitted and chopped
1 avocado, peeled, pitted, and sliced

Do Ahead Tortillas can be cooked ahead of time and refrigerated in an airtight container for up to five days.

1. Make the tortillas: In a large mixing bowl, combine the flours, salt, olive oil, and hot water. Mix with a wooden spoon, then knead by hand until the dough is smooth and elastic. Divide the dough into 9 balls. Flatten each ball into a disk between your palms. Cover with a damp kitchen towel.

2. Working with one piece at a time, roll out disks of dough between sheets of parchment paper, to form ¼-inch-thick tortillas that are 6 inches in diameter. One tortilla at a time, gently peel off the top sheet of parchment paper. Flip the tortilla, place it on a very lightly floured work surface, and peel off the second sheet.

3. Heat a large nonstick sauté pan over medium heat. Place a tortilla in the pan and cook until it just begins to brown, about 1 minute; flip and cook for another minute. Transfer to a plate and keep warm under a kitchen towel while you cook the remaining tortillas.

4. Heat a medium skillet over medium heat. Add the coconut flakes and toast, swirling the pan, until flakes are golden brown, 3 to 4 minutes.

5. In a small bowl, combine the tahini, honey, and lime juice.

6. Place the tortillas on serving plates. Divide the mango, dates, and avocado among the tortillas, and drizzle each with some of the tahini sauce. Sprinkle tops with toasted coconut flakes and serve.

Tip This tip about quinoa flour is worth repeating: instead of buying quinoa flour at the supermarket, you can make your own. The trick is to have a high-performance blender (like Breville's Boss), which can pulverize like a pro. Just put a few cups of uncooked quinoa into the blender and turn it on; within a few seconds to a minute (depending on the power of your blender), you'll have instant quinoa flour.

QUINOA TORTILLAS
WITH PEANUT-KALE BLACK RICE

If there was ever an Atkins-friendly dish that vegans and meat eaters could enjoy, it's this one. I'm a sucker for Thai-inspired peanuty sauces. With the meatiness of the kale, the nuttiness of the black rice, and the sweet peanut sauce, this is one very appealing dish.

1 cup black ("forbidden") rice
2 cups water
1 tablespoon plus 1 teaspoon peanut butter
1 tablespoon grade B organic maple syrup
2 teaspoons apple cider vinegar
½ bunch curly kale, stemmed and torn into bite-size pieces
4 Quinoa Tortillas (page 109), warmed
1 tablespoon toasted peanuts, crushed

1. In a medium pot, combine the rice with the water. Cover and bring to a boil, then lower the heat to a simmer and cook until the water is absorbed, 35 to 40 minutes. Turn the heat off and let the rice steam, covered. Allow to come to room temperature and fluff with a fork.

2. In a small microwavable bowl, stir together the peanut butter, maple syrup, and vinegar. Microwave on high for 25 to 30 seconds, and stir again.

3. In a large bowl, drizzle the dressing over the kale. Using your hands, massage the dressing into the kale; the kale will wilt and soften. Stir in the rice.

4. Divide the rice filling among the tortillas and sprinkle with the peanuts.

Do Ahead The rice can be cooked one day in advance; let the rice come to room temperature before using.

Tip The average home uses almost $2,000 worth of energy every year. The kitchen microwave can be a fast and energy-efficient way to heat foods, as it is significantly more economical than turning on the stove. For melting foods, warming them, or even just boiling water, the microwave is the greenest way to go.

QUINOA TORTILLAS WITH MUHAMMARA, SCRAMBLED EGGS, AND FRIED HALLOUMI

One of my "shame foods" was scrambled eggs and American cheese in a white flour tortilla wrap. The Natural Gourmet Institute staged an intervention, and I'm better now. I frequently whip up a batch of these Mediterranean-inflected eggs instead. Try them and you will feel better, too.

Muhammara is a zingy roasted red pepper spread of Syrian origin. It's a breeze to make your own, but store-bought will do just fine; you can find it in Middle Eastern markets or at Trader Joe's.

8 large eggs
1 teaspoon salt
1 teaspoon black pepper
1 tablespoon plus 1 teaspoon butter or coconut oil
8 ounces halloumi cheese, cut into ¼-inch slices
4 Quinoa Tortillas (page 109), warmed
4 tablespoons muhammara spread

1. In a large mixing bowl, whisk together the eggs, salt, and pepper until frothy.

2. Heat 1 tablespoon of the butter in a large nonstick skillet over medium-low heat, and pour in egg mixture. Using a silicone spatula or wooden spoon, stir the eggs from the outside in until curds begin to form, about 3 minutes. If you prefer creamier eggs, remove the skillet from the heat at this point; if you prefer a drier consistency, continue cooking for another minute.

3. Transfer the eggs to a platter and wipe the skillet clean. Return the skillet to medium heat, and add the remaining 1 teaspoon butter. Add the halloumi slices and fry until golden brown, about 1 minute; flip and brown the other side for an additional minute.

4. To serve, place the tortillas on plates and spread 1 tablespoon muhammara on each tortilla. Spoon some of the eggs onto each tortilla and top with 2 pieces of the fried cheese.

Tip If you're looking for a chemical-free alternative to conventional deodorants, you might want to steal some coconut oil from the fridge. Dabbing a little coconut oil under the arms can help neutralize body odor, because the oil naturally reduces pathogens like bacteria. It also helps moisturize and—this is the lush in me—reminds me of piña coladas.

With Muhammara, Eggs, and Halloumi

With Tropical Fruit and Tahini

With Peanut-Kale Black Rice

COCONUT WRAP

Store-bought low-carb wraps are—in a word—gross. These light wraps, in contrast, are crepe-like, with a tropical twist. Fill them to make a savory or sweet treat or do what I like to do: just eat them hot, right from the pan.

To keep these light and fluffy wraps from getting soggy, place them on a wire cooling rack as you cook them, not on a paper towel or plate. When they are cool, you can save any leftovers in a sealed freezer bag to enjoy later.

8 large egg whites
½ cup water
¼ cup coconut flour
¼ teaspoon baking powder
1 tablespoon coconut oil

1. In a mixing bowl, whisk together the egg whites, water, coconut flour, and baking powder until smooth.

2. Heat a medium skillet over medium heat. Using a pastry or silicon brush, lightly brush the skillet with coconut oil—you do not need much. Pour ⅓ cup of the batter into the hot pan, making a circle.

3. Cook until bubbles form and the wrap can move freely in the skillet or easily be pried up with a spatula, 2 to 3 minutes. The bottom should be golden brown. Flip and continue cooking until other side is also golden brown, 2 to 3 minutes more. Place cooked wraps on a cooling rack while you make the remaining wraps.

Do Ahead These wraps can be made one to two days ahead and kept in an airtight container in the refrigerator until you're ready to fill them as desired.

COCONUT WRAP WITH GRILLED SHRIMP, SCALLIONS, AND SPICY MAYO

This recipe transforms a coconut wrap into something that is just perfect for dinner and bursting with flavor. The sweetness of the wrap balances the spiciness of the shrimp and mayo. If you want to lighten up this dish, you can forgo the mayonnaise. And if you do, save it for me.

FOR THE FILLING

3 garlic cloves, minced
½-inch piece of fresh ginger, peeled and grated
3 tablespoons tamari
3 tablespoons grade B organic maple syrup
3 tablespoons apple cider vinegar
1 teaspoon salt
½ teaspoon black pepper
2 tablespoons toasted sesame oil
2 pounds large shrimp, peeled and deveined (about 30 shrimp)

FOR THE SPICY MAYO

½ cup mayonnaise
2 tablespoons Sriracha sauce (or other hot sauce)
1 teaspoon fresh lime juice (from 1 lime)

FOR THE WRAPS

6 Coconut Wraps (page 115), warmed in a skillet
1 bunch scallions, white and green parts, trimmed and thinly sliced on the diagonal
¼ cup fresh cilantro leaves
Lime wedges

1. Make the filling. In a large bowl, whisk together the garlic, ginger, tamari, maple syrup, vinegar, salt, pepper, and sesame oil. Add the shrimp and toss to coat. Cover with plastic wrap and refrigerate for 30 minutes.

2. Before cooking, allow the shrimp to come to room temperature, about 15 minutes.

3. Place a nonstick skillet over medium heat. Add the shrimp in a single layer and cook, flipping once or twice, until they curl and become firm, about 5 minutes. Be careful not to overcrowd the skillet; cook in two batches if needed.

4. Prepare the spicy mayo. In a small bowl, stir together the mayonnaise, hot sauce, and lime juice. Taste and adjust the seasonings, if necessary.

5. To serve, spread the wraps with some of the spicy mayo and top each with 4 to 6 shrimp. Sprinkle with scallions and cilantro, fold, and serve with the lime wedges.

Do Ahead The spicy mayo can be made up to two days ahead and refrigerated in an airtight container until you're ready to use it.

Good to Know Save the shrimp tails for the 15-Minute Shrimp Stock recipe on page 67.

Tip Shrimp are a sustainable seafood choice because they are fast growing and plentiful. The most sustainable shrimp is caught in Alaska, but if you can't find that at your local seafood shop or supermarket, look for a "good alternative" like shrimp from the Gulf of Mexico. But any shrimp that is certified as harvested without harming wild sea turtles is always a very good thing.

PLANTAIN TORTILLA WITH ROASTED VEGETABLES

Plantains make a great ingredient for a tortilla wrap. They are rich in dietary fiber and have more vitamin C than their cousin, the banana. If you haven't tried a plantain yet, this starchy alternative tortilla may be your thing.

FOR THE VEGETABLE FILLING

1 medium zucchini, halved or quartered
   lengthwise and cut into ½-inch pieces
1 medium yellow squash, halved lengthwise
   and cut into ½-inch pieces
1 red bell pepper, cored, seeded, and cut
   into 1-inch pieces
1 small onion, sliced
½ cup sliced organic baby carrots
8 ounces cremini mushrooms, stemmed
   and quartered
¼ cup extra-virgin olive oil
2 teaspoons salt
1 teaspoon pepper

FOR THE PLANTAIN TORTILLAS

1 large ripe yellow plantain, quartered
2 large eggs
2 teaspoons arrowroot
1 tablespoon garlic powder
1 teaspoon onion powder
1½ tablespoons melted coconut oil, plus
   more for skillet
1½ teaspoons fresh lime juice
½ teaspoon salt
½ teaspoon pepper

FOR SERVING

⅓ cup sour cream (optional)
¼ cup chopped fresh cilantro

1. Make the vegetable filling. Preheat the oven to 425°F. Line a baking sheet with parchment paper.

2. In a large bowl, toss all the vegetables with the olive oil, salt, and pepper. Spread on the prepared baking sheet and roast until the vegetables soften and turn golden brown around the edges, 25 to 30 minutes, tossing once halfway.

3. While the vegetables are roasting, make the tortillas. In a food processor, combine the plantain, eggs, arrowroot, garlic powder, onion powder, coconut oil, lime juice, salt, and pepper. Puree until smooth and creamy.

4. Heat a nonstick pan over medium heat and add about ½ teaspoon coconut oil. Add ¼ cup of the plantain batter to form a 6-inch round. Cook until bubbles begin to appear on the surface, 2 to 3 minutes, then flip and cook the other side, another 2 to 3 minutes. Remove the tortilla from the pan and keep warm while you continue making tortillas with the remaining batter. You should be able to make 4 to 6 tortillas.

5. Assemble and serve the tortillas. Combine the sour cream and cilantro in a bowl. Spread the sour cream mixture on a tortilla, top with some of the roasted vegetables, and roll up. (If not using the sour cream, simply sprinkle with the cilantro.)

Do Ahead The plantain tortillas can be prepared up to two days ahead and refrigerated in an airtight container with parchment paper between them. Reheat them to serve.

AVOCADO NORI HAND ROLLS WITH PICKLED GINGER

I don't make sushi or sashimi at home because, frankly, I don't trust myself to know if what I'm slicing is sushi grade or not. I prefer to leave it to the pros at my favorite Japanese restaurants. Hand rolls, however, are much less tricky. I gladly make this vegetarian version any day of the week.

FOR THE ROLLS

4 nori sheets
2 cups cooked short-grain brown rice
¼ cup pickled ginger, with juice
½ cup sunflower sprouts
1 avocado, peeled, pitted, and sliced
¼ cup micro greens (optional)

FOR THE DIPPING SAUCE

¼ cup tamari
¼ cup brown rice vinegar
1 teaspoon grade B organic maple syrup
¼ teaspoon red pepper flakes

1. Make the rolls. Place a nori sheet on your work surface, shiny side down. Leaving a ½-inch border from the edge of the sheet, layer ½ cup brown rice, 1 tablespoon pickled ginger, 2 tablespoons sunflower sprouts, ¼ sliced avocado, and 1 tablespoon micro greens if using. Slightly dampen the border with a bit of ginger juice, and roll up on a diagonal, away from you, tucking in the filling firmly.

2. Repeat with the remaining nori and filling to make 3 more rolls.

3. Make the dipping sauce. Combine the tamari, vinegar, maple syrup, and red pepper flakes in a small bowl; whisk to combine. Serve the dipping sauce with the hand rolls.

Tip The folks at Takaokaya—a manufacturer of seaweed nori rolls since the 1890s—say that packaged nori can be stored, if unopened, for up to six months. Once you open the package, though, it's best to transfer what you don't use to a freezer bag and store in a cool, dark place.

MASSAGED KALE AND BLACK RICE SALAD WITH PRESERVED LEMONS, DATES, AND SPICED CASHEWS

Like so many people these days, I'm kale obsessed; I find a way to work it into my lunch routine at home, abroad, or at the magazine offices. At a dude ranch shoot in Colorado, I finished my long morning horseback ride with a big bowl of kale salad (as any real cowboy would). This kale salad makes good use of leftover rice; if you don't have black ("forbidden") rice, any other variety will do.

FOR THE SALAD

1 bunch lacinato (dinosaur) kale, stemmed
   and chopped into 1- to 2-inch pieces
½ teaspoon sea salt
3 cups cooked black ("forbidden") rice, or
   other leftover rice
⅓ cup Medjool dates, pitted and chopped

FOR THE PRESERVED LEMON DRESSING

1 preserved lemon, flesh removed, chopped
½ cup avocado oil (or other flavorful oil, like
   sunflower or fruity olive)
1 teaspoon ground cumin
1 teaspoon ground coriander
2 tablespoons white balsamic vinegar
1 teaspoon grade B organic maple syrup

FOR THE SPICED CASHEWS

¾ cup cashews
1 tablespoon olive oil
1 tablespoon sumac
½ teaspoon sea salt

1. Make the salad. In a large bowl, massage the kale with the salt until tender, 1 to 2 minutes, depending how quickly and aggressively you massage; think deep tissue when rubbing. Stir in the black rice and dates.

2. Make the dressing. Blend the preserved lemon, oil, cumin, coriander, vinegar, and maple syrup until smooth in a blender or very briskly in a bowl with a whisk. Pour over the kale mixture and toss to coat.

3. Make the spiced cashews. In a dry skillet, toast the cashews, oil, sumac, and salt over medium heat for 1 minute, being careful not to burn the nuts. Sprinkle over the salad and serve.

Tip The price difference between conventional and organic kale is usually about a dollar per pound more, but it's worth it to buy organic. Conventionally grown kale can have residues of as many as forty-nine pesticides (according to a report from the USDA). Pests love kale, and so many insecticides are used to control those pests. Going organic is a surefire way to avoid these neurotoxins and carcinogens.

WARM KASHA
WITH CRISPY ROASTED POTATOES

Think of this ancient grain winner, also known as buckwheat, as comfort food without the guilt: it's low in gluten, high in fiber, and packed with protein. Just like pizza, this dish is delicious cold, the next day. Think breakfast with a fried egg right on top. Tuck in!

FOR THE POTATOES

2 Idaho baking potatoes (about 1 pound),
  cut into small dice
1 tablespoon extra-virgin olive oil
½ teaspoon salt
½ teaspoon ground pepper

FOR THE KASHA

1 teaspoon extra-virgin olive oil
½ cup kasha
¾ cup water
¼ teaspoon salt

FOR THE SAUTÉ

3 tablespoons extra-virgin olive oil
½ pound cremini mushrooms
½ teaspoon salt
1 large onion, cut into small dice
¼ cup minced garlic (about 4 cloves)
½ cup minced fresh parsley

1. Make the potatoes. Preheat the oven to 400°F. Line a rimmed baking sheet with unbleached parchment paper.

2. In a large bowl, toss together the diced potatoes, olive oil, salt, and pepper. Spread the potatoes on the prepared baking sheet in a single layer. Roast until deeply golden and crisp, approximately 45 minutes, stirring frequently.

3. Meanwhile, make the kasha. Heat the oil in a 2-quart saucepan. Add the kasha and sauté over medium heat for 2 minutes. Add the water and salt. Bring to a boil, reduce the heat to low, and cook uncovered until all the water is absorbed, about 15 minutes.

4. Make the sauté. In a 12-inch sauté pan, heat the oil. Add the mushrooms and salt, and cook the mushrooms until they release all their moisture and are well browned, about 15 minutes, stirring occasionally. Add the onion and garlic, and sauté a few minutes more, until onion is translucent.

5. Transfer the mushroom mixture to a large bowl. Add the roasted potatoes, kasha, and parsley. Toss all ingredients to combine well, then adjust seasonings, and serve.

Tip Not sure if buckwheat is right for you? Before you commit to a large bag of grain at the supermarket, get a small scoop from the bulk bin section of a local grocer and give it a spin at home. It's a good way to sample new grains economically and less wastefully.

WILTED SPINACH SALAD WITH COCONUT BACON

When I was a vegan and seemed to fraternize only with fellow plant eaters, one fact that got tossed around a lot was that Baco-Bits are vegan. The reality is, everybody loves bacon, and we missed its salty, crunchy taste. This is my ode to bacon; who knew strips of coconut could be turned into a savory, protein-packed "fakin' bacon" treat?

FOR THE COCONUT "BACON"

¼ cup large flaked coconut
½ teaspoon tamari
⅛ teaspoon smoked paprika

FOR THE DRESSING

3 tablespoons coconut oil
½ teaspoon white or black mustard seeds
2 tablespoons red wine vinegar
1 teaspoon grade B organic maple syrup
½ teaspoon Dijon mustard
Sea salt, to taste

FOR THE SALAD

4 ounces spinach (not baby, it wilts too
  quickly), stemmed, washed, and spun dry
½ pound butternut squash, peeled, diced,
  and roasted
2 ounces red onion, sliced thinly

1. Preheat the oven to 325°F. Toss together the coconut, tamari, and paprika, and bake for 10 to 15 minutes, tossing every 5 minutes. Transfer to a cool baking sheet; the "bacon" bits will crisp as they cool.

2. Make the dressing: Warm the oil and add the mustard seeds. When the seeds begin to pop, carefully add the vinegar. Whisk in the maple syrup and mustard, and season with salt.

3. Divide and arrange the spinach, squash, and red onion between two plates.

4. Drizzle the dressing over the spinach to wilt lightly, and sprinkle with the coconut "bacon."

Do Ahead The coconut bacon can be prepared up to one week in advance and refrigerated in an airtight container until ready to serve. To serve, re-crisp in a preheated 325°F oven.

COCONUT MISO-GLAZED JAPANESE EGGPLANT

This vegan glaze is both savory and sweet, which works beautifully on Japanese eggplant and other hearty vegetables. You can also substitute chicken or beef for the eggplant; use extra sauce to give these proteins a caramelized glaze.

¾ cup sake or light white wine

¼ cup seasoned rice wine (mirin)

¼ cup filtered water

6 tablespoons light/white miso

1 teaspoon agave syrup (light or dark)

1 tablespoon unrefined coconut oil

3 Japanese eggplants (approximately 1.5 pounds), sliced lengthwise from stem to end

1. Mix together the sake, mirin, water, miso, agave, and coconut oil—by hand or in a blender. Coat the eggplants and allow to marinate for 30 minutes and up to 1 hour.

2. Bring the eggplants to room temperature, wipe off any excess marinade, and grill or broil until eggplant is tender and caramelized, 10 to 12 minutes. Alternatively, roast in the oven on a baking sheet at 375°F for 15 to 20 minutes.

ACTIVE TIME 45 MINUTES
TOTAL TIME 1 HOUR 45 MINUTES
SERVES 4 TO 6

BULGUR-CHICKPEA SALAD
WITH GOLDEN BERRIES AND GOJI BERRIES

At the age of twelve, I decided to become a vegetarian. My mother told me, "If you're not going to eat the meals I make, you need to cook for yourself." So, I did. And one of the go-to "recipes" I made for myself was these chickpeas sautéed in olive oil with salt, pepper, and whatever dried herbs I found in my mother's pantry. Now, this recipe is my grown-up version: it's bright, fresh, and savory and sweet. I still love it, and I think you will, too.

2 cups water

½ teaspoon salt

1 cup bulgur

2 teaspoons ground cumin

1½ teaspoons ground coriander

½ teaspoon ground cinnamon

¼ cup extra-virgin olive oil

Zest and juice of ½ lemon, plus additional zest for garnish (optional)

¼ teaspoon freshly ground black pepper

1 (15-ounce) can chickpeas, drained and rinsed

4 scallions, white and green parts, chopped

1 tablespoon chopped fresh mint

½ cup golden berries, roughly chopped

¼ cup goji berries

1. In a medium pot, bring the water to a boil with ¼ teaspoon of the salt. Stir in the bulgur, cover, turn the heat off, and let the pot stand until all the water is absorbed, about 30 minutes.

2. Meanwhile, in a small dry skillet, toast the cumin, coriander, and cinnamon, stirring constantly with a wooden spoon, until fragrant, 2 to 3 minutes. Transfer to a plate to cool.

3. In a bowl, whisk together the olive oil, lemon juice and zest, black pepper, and remaining ¼ teaspoon salt.

4. When ready, toss the bulgur with the toasted spices. Add the chickpeas, scallions, mint, golden berries, and goji berries. Add the dressing and toss to mix. Cover with plastic wrap and refrigerate for 30 minutes. Taste and re-season before serving, if needed.

use your head

Like broccoli and kale, cauliflower is a cruciferous vegetable that contains sulforaphane, a powerful plant compound that has shown cancer-fighting potential in numerous studies. One cup of chopped cauliflower has a whopping 85 percent of your daily vitamin C and 11 grams of protein. But what we love most about this humble superfood is how cheap and versatile it is. A head of the stuff will usually cost you less than $4 (by the way, although it's often white, you may also see it in hues like purple and orange, especially at the farmer's market). Cauliflower is also on the Environmental Working Group's "Clean Fifteen" list of produce that's least likely to have pesticide contamination. Look for cauliflower that's firm (mushy florets and brown spots indicate it's started to spoil). The leaves should be crisp, not slimy or wilted. The best way to store it is in the crisper in a perforated plastic bag.

Think of cauliflower as a blank canvas: There are countless ways to incorporate it into savory and sweet dishes. You can sear it like steak, grind it up into "rice," and even sneak it into brownies to add creaminess and a dose of filling protein.

GOOD TO KNOW ABOUT CAULIFLOWER

1. Cauliflower leaves are edible! They're especially good roasted in the oven until they're browned and crunchy, the way you'd make kale chips.

2. The head of the cauliflower is known as a "curd" and is made up of undeveloped white flower buds (technically they're called inflorescence meristems).

3. Orange cauliflower—sometimes called cheddar cauliflower—gets its color because it has extra beta-carotene. As a result, it has about 25 times more vitamin A than regular cauliflower. Orange cauliflower also has a milder, sweeter taste.

4. There are just 25 calories and 5 grams of carbs in one cup of cauliflower.

5. Don't freeze cauliflower (it tends to emerge mushy), unless you're going to make a puree with it. Before freezing, trim the head into florets and blanch them for 3 minutes.

CAST-IRON SEARED CAULIFLOWER STEAK

I've never been one to really obsess over calories, but this is a fact that's hard to ignore: 1 cup of cauliflower is just 25 calories. The "meatiest" of vegetables, one of my favorite ways to eat it is to sear it like a steak and drizzle chimichurri sauce on top. Served with the smoothie of your choice, this is a healthy and satisfying lunch or light dinner.

¼ cup avocado oil

1 head cauliflower, cut into ½-inch-thick vertical slices

½ teaspoon sea salt

Freshly ground black pepper

FOR THE CHIMICHURRI

1 bunch parsley, destemmed

1 bunch cilantro, destemmed

2 garlic cloves, chopped

¼ cup red wine vinegar

½ teaspoon sea salt

¼ teaspoon red chili flakes

¾ cup olive oil

1. Preheat the oven to 375°F. Heat a large cast-iron pan over high heat.

2. Add the oil, sprinkle the cauliflower slabs with salt and pepper, and cook for 2 to 4 minutes per side, or until golden and crispy.

3. Transfer the pan to the oven and cook for an additional 10 minutes, or until the cauliflower is tender.

4. To make the chimichurri, combine the parsley, cilantro, garlic, vinegar, salt, and red chili flakes in a food processor and pulse lightly. Stream in the olive oil and process until smooth.

5. Spoon the chimichurri over the cauliflower to serve.

CHAPTER FIVE

here's dinner!

When I started *Naturally, Danny Seo*, we began the development process of determining "who are we" by poring over the pages of other magazines on the newsstand. We went through dozens of food, lifestyle, and general interest publications and came to this conclusion: very few of us will ever have an antique harvest table, set amid a field of golden wildflowers on which we serve our perfectly behaved (and styled) children gorgeously plated food as the sun sets to a majestic reddish hue.

Magazines are meant to be dreamy and aspirational, but the reality is that most of us are rushing home from work, picking up the kids from soccer practice or ballet class, and generally have to MacGyver our way through the kitchen to turn scant ingredients into a family-friendly meal. It's no wonder take-out and frozen entrees from Costco, along with a ripped-open bag of pre-washed organic greens tossed with bottled salad dressing, often win out. The truth is, convenience can trump all. And it's been my mission in the pages of our magazine to make healthy food fast, fresh, and easy.

So, for this chapter—the heart of weeknight cooking—I wanted to mix it up: make use of convenient appliances like slow cookers and seasonal ingredients, as well as things that could be go-to's when there's just a *bit* more time and some epicurean delights that could be whipped up for special occasions or on the weekends.

Many of these dishes can be made in big batches, frozen, or simply reheated and enjoyed again the next day. To round them out, make your own sides: a massaged kale salad, simply roasted vegetables, or fresh tomatoes sprinkled with salt and cracked black peppercorns.

Here's dinner!

ACTIVE TIME 15 MINUTES
TOTAL TIME 7 HOURS 15 MINUTES
SERVES 8

winter slow cooker
BRAISED GRASS-FED BEEF RAGÙ WITH CREAMY POLENTA

Before you walk away from this recipe after noting a total time of 7 hours and 15 minutes, please take a second look: you'll actually devote only 15 minutes of active time to make this luscious, filling, and oh-so-good winter pick-me-up. The reason this is so is the good old-fashioned slow cooker. Just fill it up in the morning and walk away. And just about when it's time for an early dinner, you just have to pop open a bottle of organic wine, toss a salad, and there you have it: dinner.

FOR THE BRAISED BEEF

2 tablespoons extra-virgin olive oil

2¼ pounds grass-fed boneless beef round

2 teaspoons salt

½ teaspoon black pepper

1 large onion, diced (about 1½ cups)

12 ounces cremini mushrooms, stemmed and quartered

4 small carrots, cut into ½-inch slices

3 garlic cloves, minced

1 (28-ounce) can whole peeled tomatoes with juice

½ cup dry red wine

3 tablespoons tomato paste

1 teaspoon dried basil

1 teaspoon dried oregano

2 bay leaves

FOR THE POLENTA

6 cups water and/or broth

1⅓ cups yellow cornmeal

1 teaspoon salt

3 tablespoons grated Parmesan cheese

2 tablespoons chopped fresh parsley

1. Prepare the beef. In a large skillet, heat the olive oil over medium heat. Season the beef with salt and pepper, and add it to the skillet, browning on all sides, about 5 minutes per side.

2. In a 4-quart slow cooker, combine the onion, mushrooms, carrots, garlic, tomatoes, wine, tomato paste, basil, oregano, and bay leaves; nestle the beef into the mixture, then cover and cook on low heat for 7 hours.

3. Allow the meat to rest for 1 hour.

4. While the meat is resting, prepare the polenta. In a medium pot, bring the water to a boil with the salt. While continually whisking, gradually stir in the cornmeal. Continue to stir for 5 minutes to eliminate any lumps. Lower the heat, cover, and simmer the polenta until it is creamy and cooked through, 40 to 45 minutes.

5. Transfer the beef to a large cutting board. Using two forks, shred the meat and stir it back into the sauce.

6. Stir the Parmesan into the polenta. Serve immediately, with the meaty sauce, sprinkled with the parsley.

Good to Know Instant polenta is just as good as the long-cooked type, in my opinion, so if you want to make a creamy polenta in a few minutes, go right ahead.

spring slow cooker
JERK CHICKEN WITH CARIBBEAN SALSA

Here's another slow cooker jam, one that will take you to the island-nation of Jamaica. When you can, buy organic chicken raised without antibiotics and allowed only organic grains. Chickens that are raised organically have the ability to graze for things that taste good to them, like bugs and seeds. Fortunately, what tastes good to the chickens also leads to good-tasting meat.

FOR THE CHICKEN

1½ pounds boneless, skinless chicken thighs
3 garlic cloves, minced
¼ cup fresh orange juice
1 teaspoon dried thyme
½ teaspoon ground cinnamon
Pinch of ground allspice
Pinch of ground nutmeg
¼ teaspoon red pepper flakes
¼ teaspoon ground turmeric
2 teaspoons grade B organic maple syrup
1 cup chicken stock
1 tablespoon apple cider vinegar
2 teaspoons tomato paste
2 tablespoons fresh lime juice
½ teaspoon salt
¼ teaspoon freshly ground black pepper
2 tablespoons chopped fresh chives
 (optional)

FOR THE CARIBBEAN SALSA

1 small mango, peeled, pitted, and diced
⅓ pineapple, peeled, cored, and diced
1 small red onion, finely diced (about ⅓ cup)
Juice of 1 lime (about 2 tablespoons)
2 tablespoons chopped fresh chives
1 tablespoon extra-virgin olive oil
½ teaspoon salt, or more as needed

1. Start the chicken. Place all the ingredients in a 4-quart slow cooker. Stir to combine. Cover and cook on the low setting for 8 hours.

2. While the chicken is cooking, prepare the salsa. In a bowl, combine the ingredients. Cover with plastic wrap and refrigerate until ready to serve. Taste and season with additional salt, if needed.

3. Transfer the chicken to a large work surface. Using two forks, shred the chicken. Return the chicken meat to the pot and stir into the sauce.

4. Serve the chicken in bowls, topped with the salsa and a sprinkle of chives if you like.

Do Ahead The chicken can be made up to two days ahead and refrigerated until ready to serve. The salsa can be made up to one day ahead.

Tip If you're slicing up a whole pineapple to get 1½ cups of fruit for this recipe, save the rest for smoothies. Just freeze the leftover pineapple on a baking sheet and then transfer to sealable plastic bags. Add a few chunks to the blender to give your morning smoothie a sweet vibe.

summer slow cooker
LOW 'N' SLOW SEAFOOD BOIL

I don't eat meat, so when I make this seafood boil, I use vegan sausage made from Tofurky instead of the turkey sausage. I sauté the sausage and add it at the end to give the boil the smoky, meaty flavor that makes it so good. With either kind of sausage, though, this is a satisfying bowl of goodness, perfect for a summer gathering.

8 cups water

2 (12-ounce) bottles amber lager (one for the boil, one for you)

6 garlic cloves, minced

2 tablespoons Old Bay seasoning

1 tablespoon ground cumin

1 teaspoon salt

½ teaspoon freshly ground black pepper

½ teaspoon smoked paprika

2 pounds red potatoes, scrubbed and quartered (about 6 potatoes)

6 celery stalks, cut into 1-inch pieces

2 medium onions, quartered

2 lemons, halved

4 ears of corn, shucked and each cut into 4 pieces

1 pound smoked turkey or chicken sausage, cut into ¾-inch slices

2 pounds large shrimp, peeled and deveined

2 tablespoons chopped fresh parsley

2 tablespoons chopped scallions, white and green parts

1 baguette, cut into 1-inch slices and lightly grilled

1. In a 4- or 5-quart slow cooker, stir together the water, 1 bottle of beer, the garlic, Old Bay seasoning, cumin, salt, pepper, and paprika. Add the potatoes, celery, onions, and lemons. Cover and cook on the low setting until the vegetables are tender, about 3 hours.

2. Add the corn and sausage, and cook for 2 more hours.

3. Turn the heat level to high and add the shrimp. Cook for another 30 minutes.

4. Serve the stew garnished with the parsley and scallions, and accompany with crusty bread.

Tip When checking out your purchases at the grocery store, it's important to separate certain foods from others to avoid cross contamination in your reusable bags. According to FoodSafety.gov, you should keep all meat products, poultry, seafood, and eggs away from the rest of the food. The juices from the raw meat can drip onto other items and spread harmful bacteria. And always be sure to bring your perishable groceries home right away, and to store them away from direct sunlight in the car to keep them as cool as possible.

fall slow cooker
VEGETARIAN CURRY
WITH SWEET POTATOES AND CHICKPEAS

Inspired by my travels to India, this hearty vegetarian curry can be scooped onto a bed of fluffy brown rice or quinoa. As curries go, it is on the milder end of the heat index, so for those of you who love really spicy food, you can amp it up with chiles and red pepper flakes.

1 head cauliflower, cut into florets (about 4 cups)

2 sweet potatoes, peeled and cut into large chunks

1 red bell pepper, cored, seeded, and roughly diced

1 large onion, diced

1 (15-ounce) can chickpeas, rinsed and drained

1 (15-ounce) can whole peeled tomatoes

4 ounces frozen peas

4 ounces full-fat coconut milk

½ cup low-sodium vegetable broth

1 tablespoon ground cumin

1 tablespoon curry powder

1 tablespoon ground turmeric

1 teaspoon salt

½ teaspoon cayenne pepper

¼ teaspoon freshly ground black pepper

2 tablespoons chopped scallions, white and green parts

2 tablespoons fresh cilantro leaves

2 tablespoons fresh mint, cut in thin ribbons

1. In a 4-quart slow cooker, combine the cauliflower, sweet potatoes, red pepper, onion, chickpeas, tomatoes, peas, coconut milk, broth, cumin, curry powder, turmeric, salt, cayenne, and black pepper.

2. Cover and cook on the low setting until the vegetables are tender, about 8 hours.

3. Serve garnished with the scallions, cilantro, and mint.

Do Ahead The prepared curry will keep in the fridge for up to three days.

Tip Turmeric can stain very easily. If you get it on fabric, don't reach for laundry detergent and saturate it. Laundry detergent is strong stuff and can break down the fibers of whatever it is you're pre-treating. Instead, use liquid dish detergent as a spot treater. The dish detergent is designed to gently remove stains and grease, and it will lift the stain out of the fabric. Soak the stained fabric in cold water, generously apply the dish detergent, and let it sit for an hour before rinsing clean.

anytime slow cooker
BALSAMIC BRAISED BEEF SHANKS

Prime cuts of grass-fed, organic beef can be expensive, so this recipe is a budget winner. Inexpensive beef shank comes from the leg of the cow, which means it is tough and chewy muscle. Slow braising tenderizes the meat, which literally falls off the bone when it's ready to eat. Serve this hearty dish with creamy polenta, coconut oil–braised greens, or oven-roasted veggies for a complete and comforting meal.

1 tablespoon sea salt

1 tablespoon dried rosemary

1 tablespoon dried sage

1 tablespoon garlic powder

1 tablespoon onion powder

1 tablespoon paprika

1 teaspoon ground black pepper

½ teaspoon cayenne pepper

4 beef shanks, about 2 pounds

1 tablespoon extra-virgin olive oil

1 (15-ounce) can tomato sauce

½ cup balsamic vinegar

4 dried dates, pitted and halved

6 garlic cloves, smashed

1. In a small bowl, mix the salt, rosemary, sage, garlic powder, onion powder, paprika, black pepper, and cayenne. Rinse the beef shank pieces and pat dry, then rub with the spice mix on all sides.

2. In a large sauté pan, heat the oil over medium-high heat. Sear the meat for 2 to 3 minutes per side, until browned all over.

3. In a slow cooker, combine the tomato sauce, vinegar, dates, and garlic. Add the seared ribs and spoon the mixture over the ribs to coat well. Cover, and cook on low heat for 4 to 6 hours, until the meat is tender.

4. Serve alongside the starch of your choice: rice, noodles, or baked or mashed potatoes.

Tip Choosing unconventional cuts of meat is one way to help curb food waste. Did you know that to make one pound of ground beef, it takes 2,500 gallons of water? That's forty times more water than is needed to produce a pound of potatoes.

BRAISED OXTAILS
WITH ORANGES AND DATES

Oxtails are rich in gelatin, which makes them well suited to preparations involving long, slow cooking. This recipe works well in a slow cooker, too, but you should brown the meat in a heavy-bottomed pan before moving it to the slow cooker. That browning makes a big difference in the meat's texture and flavor, yet takes only a few extra minutes.

3 pounds oxtails, in 1-inch lengths

1 teaspoon salt

½ teaspoon black pepper

Flour, for dusting

3 tablespoons extra-virgin olive oil

2 medium onions, diced

2 large carrots, cut into ½-inch pieces

4 sprigs fresh thyme

1 tablespoon tomato paste

¼ teaspoon ground cloves

1½ cups dry red wine

2 cups beef broth

Zest and juice of 1 orange, plus more for garnish

1 cup pitted Medjool dates

1 tablespoon chopped fresh parsley

1. Season the oxtails on both sides with salt and pepper, and dust lightly with flour.

2. In a Dutch oven or heavy-bottomed saucepan, heat 2 tablespoons of the olive oil over medium heat. Add the oxtails and sear on all sides until browned, 2 to 3 minutes. Be careful not to overcrowd the pan; sear oxtails in batches, if needed. Transfer the oxtails to a platter.

3. Add the remaining 1 tablespoon olive oil to the pan and add the onions, carrots, and thyme. Cook until the onions are slightly browned and carrots are tender, stirring occasionally, about 5 minutes. Stir in the tomato paste and cloves.

4. Return the oxtails to the pan and add the wine, beef broth, orange peel, and dates. Bring to a boil, cover with a lid, turn heat down to low, and braise until the meat pulls away from the bone, about 3 hours.

5. Using tongs or a slotted spoon, pull out the oxtail bones and discard. Serve sprinkled with the parsley and orange zest.

Do Ahead The dish can be prepared up to two days ahead and reheated.

SHAKE-AND-BAKE ETHIOPIAN CHICKEN AND LENTILS

This flavorful dinner is a protein powerhouse. If you can't find the lacinato kale, any other hearty green, like collards or Swiss chard, will work beautifully, too.

The Berber spice mix is nice to have it on hand to season grains, veggies, and all types of proteins, as well as seeds, nuts, and chickpeas.

FOR THE BERBER SPICE

2 teaspoons cayenne pepper
1½ teaspoons sea salt
1½ teaspoons ground cumin
1½ teaspoons ground coriander
1½ teaspoons paprika
½ teaspoon ground black pepper
½ teaspoon ground ginger
½ teaspoon ground cardamom
¼ teaspoon ground cloves
¼ teaspoon ground turmeric

FOR THE LENTILS

1 tablespoon coconut oil
3 garlic cloves, minced
1 red onion, chopped
1 teaspoon salt
1 cup red lentils
2 to 2½ cups water
1 tablespoon Berber spice
½ cup tomato puree
1 bunch lacinato (dinosaur) kale, stemmed
  and roughly chopped

FOR THE CHICKEN

2 pounds boneless, skinless chicken breasts
2 cups almond meal
¼ cup coconut flour
About ⅓ cup coconut oil

1. Make the Berber spice mix. In a small bowl, stir together all the spices.

2. Make the lentils. Heat the coconut oil in a large sauté pan over medium heat. Add the garlic and cook until fragrant, about 1 minute. Add the onion and salt, and cook until the onion is softened, 3 to 5 minutes.

3. Stir in the lentils. Add the water, 1 tablespoon of the Berber spice, and tomato puree. Cover the pan and simmer, stirring frequently, until the lentils are cooked through, about 20 minutes. Stir in the kale and cook until just wilted, about 2 minutes more.

4. While the lentils are cooking, cut the chicken into 2-inch pieces. In a large brown paper bag, combine the chicken with 2 tablespoons of the Berber spice, the almond meal, and coconut flour. Close the bag and shake until the chicken is coated with the mixture.

5. Heat 2 tablespoons of the coconut oil in a large nonstick skillet over medium heat. Cook the chicken (in batches, if needed, adding more oil as necessary; do not overcrowd the pan) until golden brown on all sides, 6 to 7 minutes.

6. To serve, divide the lentil-kale mixture among plates and top with chicken.

GARLIC-GINGER MULLET
WITH VEGETABLES EN PAPILLOTE

Here's a very fancy French way of saying that this dinner is all cooked in paper. Parchment paper to be more exact. I like making this dish at home, when I'm cooking for a crowd. The portions of protein and vegetables are self-contained in their own pouches and steaming helps keep the flesh moist and tender. Just remember to use unbleached parchment paper, which is chlorine-free.

If you are unable to find mullet, artic char makes a nice alternative.

A 4-inch piece of fresh ginger, peeled and minced
6 garlic cloves, minced
2 tablespoons toasted sesame oil
2 tablespoons tamari
2 tablespoons rice vinegar
2 tablespoons mirin
2 tablespoons honey
4 scallions, white and green parts, trimmed and julienned or chopped
4 (8-ounce) skinless mullet fillets
1½ cups shiitake mushrooms, stemmed and thinly sliced
1 yellow bell pepper, cored, seeded, and thinly sliced
1 pint grape tomatoes, halved
1 small zucchini, thinly sliced
Sea salt and black pepper

1. In a medium bowl, whisk together the ginger, garlic, sesame oil, tamari, rice vinegar, mirin, honey, and scallions. Place the mullet fillets in a shallow dish and cover with the marinade. Refrigerate for 20 minutes, flipping the fillets in the marinade after 10 minutes.

2. Preheat the oven to 400°F.

3. In a large bowl, toss together the mushrooms, yellow pepper, tomatoes, and zucchini. Set aside.

4. Fold four 14 by 12-inch pieces of parchment paper in half. Using scissors, cut the paper into a heart shape. Unfold the hearts and place an equal amount of vegetables on one side of each heart. Top each with a mullet fillet and season with salt and pepper. Fold the second half of the parchment over the filling. Starting with a point of the heart, make small folds around the edge to form a sealed packet.

5. Place the packets on a baking sheet and bake for 20 minutes.

6. Remove from the oven and unwrap the hot packets carefully, using kitchen shears to make a slit in the parchment. The fish should be opaque. Serve immediately.

ACTIVE TIME 20 MINUTES
TOTAL TIME 50 MINUTES
MAKES 16 TO 20 SKEWERS
SERVES 6 TO 8

MEXICAN SHRIMP SKEWERS

While all of the recipes in this book are really tasty, this is one I seem to go back to over and over again at home. It's that good. In fact, I love this DIY spice mix so much that I make large batches of it and store it in glass jars, ready to spice up cubes of firm tofu, seitan, and tempeh. I even add it to scrambled eggs to give them a little kick before I fold the eggs into a brown rice tortilla for a quick on-the-go breakfast.

FOR THE SPICE MIX

3 tablespoons ground cumin
1 tablespoon plus 1 teaspoon garlic powder
1 tablespoon ground coriander
1 tablespoon cayenne pepper
1 tablespoon smoked paprika
1 tablespoon dried oregano
1 tablespoon onion powder

FOR THE SKEWERS

3 pounds large shrimp, peeled and deveined, rinsed and patted dry
½ cup extra-virgin olive oil
6 garlic cloves, minced
Zest and juice of 2 limes
2 teaspoons salt
1 teaspoon freshly ground black pepper
1 cup chopped fresh cilantro (about ½ bunch)
16 ounces cremini mushrooms, stemmed and halved
2 red bell peppers, cored, seeded, and cut into 2-inch pieces
2 zucchini, halved lengthwise and cut into ½-inch-thick pieces
2 pints cherry tomatoes

Plus: 20 wooden skewers, soaked in water for at least 20 minutes

1. Make the spice mix. In a large bowl, whisk together the ingredients.
2. Prepare the skewers. Add the shrimp to the spice mix and toss to coat. Cover with plastic wrap and refrigerate for 20 minutes.
3. Preheat the oven to 350°F. Line a baking sheet with parchment paper.
4. Meanwhile, whisk together the oil, garlic, lime zest and juice, salt, pepper, and ½ cup of the cilantro. Toss in the mushrooms, red peppers, zucchini, and tomatoes.
5. When ready, skewer the shrimp and vegetables, and place on the prepared baking sheet. Drizzle with any remaining oil from the vegetable bowl. Bake until the shrimp are no longer translucent, 15 to 20 minutes.
6. Serve the skewers garnished with remaining ½ cup cilantro.

SAFFRON CAULIFLOWER "RICE" PAELLA

We're often told by nutritionists to avoid "white" foods, but cauliflower is a huge exception. It's a cruciferous vegetable (just like broccoli, kale, and Brussels sprouts), so it contains a powerful plant compound called sulforaphane that has been shown in numerous studies to have cancer-fighting potential. Health benefits aside, cauliflower's sweet, nutty flavor works in a wide variety of recipes. I love this paella because it's fast to make and low in carbs—and delicious.

1 head cauliflower (about 4 cups florets)
¼ cup olive oil
1 teaspoon sea salt
1 yellow onion, diced
4 garlic cloves, minced
1 can whole tomatoes, crushed
2 cups vegetable stock
½ teaspoon saffron
½ pound shrimp
½ pound mussels
1 cup frozen peas, defrosted
1 bunch parsley leaves, chopped
2 lemons, cut into wedges for serving

1. Remove the cauliflower stalks and pulse the florets in a food processor.

2. Preheat the oil in a large pan over medium heat. Add the cauliflower and salt and sauté for 5 minutes, or until golden.

3. Add the onion and cook for an additional few minutes, or until translucent. Add the garlic and cook for an additional minute.

4. Fold in the tomatoes, stock, and saffron and bring to a simmer. Add the shrimp and mussels, cover, and cook for 5 minutes, or until the shellfish is cooked through. (Discard any mussels that have not opened.)

5. Turn off the heat. Fold in the peas and parsley. Serve with lemon wedges on the side.

GLAZED EGGPLANT AND BLACK SESAME FRIED RICE

Whenever I make rice at home, I prepare a double batch and use the leftover to scatter on salads or make a quick-and-easy stir-fry. Brown rice has become one of my favorites because it's nutty and is a star leftover ingredient. It's also good for you: gluten free, high in fiber and iron, and full of antioxidants. If you don't have a wok, a cast-iron skillet would work well, but really, any other hot skillet would do.

You can find shichimi togarashi, a common Japanese seven-spice mixture, in any Asian supermarket. Think of it as the Asian Mrs. Dash!

½ cup toasted sesame oil

2 Japanese eggplants, trimmed and cut lengthwise into 1-inch strips

¼ cup soy sauce or tamari

¼ cup grade B organic maple syrup

3 cups cooked long-grain brown rice

¼ cup chopped scallions, white and green parts

2 tablespoons shichimi togarashi

2 tablespoons black sesame seeds

4 large eggs, fried (optional)

1. Preheat a wok over high heat. Add half the sesame oil and when hot, add the eggplant. Cook, stirring constantly, for 3 to 5 minutes, or until eggplant is golden and softened. Add the soy sauce and maple syrup, and stir to deglaze the pan. Remove eggplant from the wok and keep warm.

2. Reheat the wok over high heat. Add the remaining ¼ cup sesame oil, and when oil is warm, add the rice and stir for 2 minutes, or until the rice is hot and starts crisping up. Fold in the scallions and shichimi togarashi, and cook for an additional minute, gently tossing with a wooden spoon or spatula.

3. To serve, mound the rice on serving dishes. Place the eggplant on top, and sprinkle with the sesame seeds. Top each serving with a fried egg, if desired.

Tip If you've purchased a new wok, give it a thorough cleaning when you get it home. Most new woks with that shiny factory finish have been sprayed with oil to prevent rust. This finish needs to be washed off with hot, soapy water. Then season your new wok as you normally would.

WHOLE WHEAT FETTUCCINE WITH ALMOND CREAM SAUCE AND SUN-DRIED TOMATOES

Everybody loves pasta, but it seems not everybody can eat the same kind of pasta. If you're looking to cut your carbs or can't tolerate gluten, you can make this dish with one of the many alternative pastas available at health food stores. Brown rice, corn, black bean, and lentil pastas are all good gluten-free options. But if you can eat wheat, do it. Man, oh, man—wheat pasta never tastes so good when you make it with this creamy vegan sauce.

While the water comes to a boil and the pasta cooks, get started on assembling the sauce. Just remember that the pasta must be hot when it gets tossed in the sauce, otherwise the sauce won't coat it as well.

1 head of garlic
¾ cup extra-virgin olive oil
1 cup almond meal
2 tablespoons soy or chickpea miso
½ teaspoon black pepper
1 pound whole wheat fettuccine
½ cup sun-dried tomatoes, thinly sliced
10–20 fresh basil leaves
¼ cup slivered almonds, toasted

1. Preheat the oven to 375°F.

2. Trim off the top one-fourth of the garlic, exposing the cloves while keeping the head intact. Place on a square of aluminum foil, drizzle with 2 tablespoons of the oil, and wrap up, connecting the four corners of foil at the top to create a packet. Roast for 30 minutes. Unwrap and set aside to cool.

3. Once it's cool enough to handle, squeeze the garlic cloves from their skins into a food processor. Add the almond meal, miso, pepper, and ½ cup olive oil. Puree until smooth.

4. Bring 4 quarts of water to a boil. Add the fettuccine and cook until cooked through but still chewy, about 10 minutes. Reserve 1½ cups of the pasta cooking water, then drain the pasta. Transfer the pasta back to the pot and toss with the remaining 2 tablespoons olive oil.

5. With the food processor motor running, stream some of the pasta cooking water into the almond sauce. The sauce should be the consistency of Alfredo sauce, so add only enough water to achieve that thickness; you may need only a few tablespoons.

6. Using tongs, toss the pasta with the almond sauce and add the sun-dried tomatoes. Transfer the pasta to a serving bowl and garnish with the basil and almonds.

CREAMY BASIL-SPINACH PESTO

It's smart to have a few go-to sauce recipes so you can dress up whatever pantry staples you have on hand. I've learned to keep cubes of this pesto in my freezer; when I come home from a cross-country flight, I boil up a little gluten-free pasta, toss in a few pesto cubes, and tuck into a big bowl of Welcome Home deliciousness.

This vegan pesto is perfect with pasta, potatoes, fish, and chicken—or to spread on bread when building a sandwich at home. If it doesn't say "pesto" to you without the cheese, swap out the miso and umeboshi paste for a few tablespoons of good grated Parmesan cheese.

1 large bunch fresh basil (about 2 cups packed leaves)
2 cups packed baby spinach
2 garlic cloves
1 cup raw cashews
1 teaspoon soy or chickpea miso
½ teaspoon umeboshi paste
¼ teaspoon ground black pepper
¼ teaspoon red pepper flakes
¼ teaspoon salt
½ cup extra-virgin olive oil

Combine the basil, spinach, garlic, cashews, miso, umeboshi paste, pepper, red pepper flakes, and salt in a food processor, and pulse to combine. With the motor running, slowly stream in the olive oil and puree until creamy. Taste and season with more salt, if needed.

CRISPY RICE SUSHI
WITH SRIRACHA AÏOLI AND SASHIMI

This is a recipe that ran in the pages of *Naturally*; it was inspired by famed chef Jean-Georges Vongerichten and his equally famous fried sushi cakes.

This is probably the best argument for always making a double batch of rice: it transforms last night's leftovers into an (almost) five-star delight. The rice is crispy and crunchy (but soft and wonderful inside) when fried as cakes; and the aïoli adds just enough heat and creaminess to make each bite delectable. (To save time, simply mix your favorite store-bought aïoli with Sriracha.) You can top the sushi cakes with thin slices of sushi-grade fish, but I have found slices of avocado to be just as delicious.

FOR THE AÏOLI

1 large egg yolk
1 large egg
Juice of 1 lemon
1 teaspoon Dijon mustard
1 teaspoon sea salt
1 cup avocado oil
2 tablespoons Sriracha, or to taste

FOR THE SUSHI

2 cups cooked short-grain brown rice
½ cup hot water
3 tablespoons ponzu (a Japanese citrus sauce, available in the Asian section of your grocery store)
¼ cup arrowroot
½ cup coconut oil
¼ pound wild-caught mackerel (or favorite sustainable sashimi, like yellowfin tuna or kingfish), sliced
Micro greens, for garnish

1. Make the aïoli. Combine the egg yolk and whole egg, lemon juice, mustard, and salt in a food processor, and pulse until combined. Slowly stream in the oil while the motor is running. Transfer to a bowl and fold in the hot sauce. Refrigerate until ready to serve.

2. Line a 13-inch square baking dish with plastic wrap.

3. Make the sushi. Combine the rice with the hot water and ponzu and spread in a 1-inch layer in the prepared baking pan. Press firmly into the pan, cover, and refrigerate for 1 hour, or until firm.

4. Spread the arrowroot on a plate. Using a hot knife, cut the chilled rice into rectangles or other shapes. Dredge the rice cakes in the arrowroot.

5. Preheat the oil in a large pan and cook the rice cakes until golden, 2 to 4 minutes per side.

6. To serve, place a dollop of aïoli on each crisp rice cake. Arrange a piece of mackerel on top, and garnish with the greens.

make rice
LIKE A PRO

Sure, those microwaveable bags of rice are quick and convenient, but buying a big bag of rice or getting it from the bulk bin will save you a lot of money—and you'll be tossing out fewer plastic bags, too. But once you see how easy (and better tasting!) it is to make your own, you'll never go back to pre-cooked.

To keep rice from sticking to the pan, use a heavy-bottomed pan that distributes heat evenly, and cook over low heat. Keep the pan covered while cooking and resist the urge to stir a lot. You can check on the rice's progress by tilting the pan to the side to see if any water remains.

- For added flavor, toast the rice before cooking it. Pour a small amount of fat into a pan and cook the rice for a few minutes until it's golden brown and aromatic.

- Long-grain rice is best when you want fluffy, pilaf-like results. For stickier dishes (sushi, risotto), use shorter grains.

- Use stock, wine, or whole spices like cinnamon sticks, lemongrass, or kaffir lime leaves for an added infusion of flavor.

- You don't have to cook rice on the stovetop. Baking is a great option too, especially if you're making a large batch.

ACTIVE TIME 15 MINUTES
TOTAL TIME 15 MINUTES
MAKES 1½ CUPS

RED CURRY PEANUT SAUCE

This simple Asian-inspired sauce is a creamy and tasty way to dress up instant rice noodles, rice, vegetables, and all types of protein, from chicken to tofu. Look for Thai curry paste in the international section of your supermarket or go to an Asian market.

2 tablespoons toasted sesame oil
1 small shallot, diced
2 garlic cloves, minced
2 tablespoons Thai red curry paste
2 tablespoons grade B organic maple syrup
¾ cup creamy natural-style peanut butter
1 (14-ounce) can full-fat coconut milk
2 tablespoons mirin
2 tablespoons lime juice (from 1 lime)
2 tablespoons chopped toasted peanuts

1. In a small saucepan, heat the sesame oil over medium-low heat. Add the shallot and garlic, and cook until soft, about 1 minute.

2. Add the curry paste, maple syrup, peanut butter, coconut milk, and mirin; whisk until smooth. Bring to a boil, then reduce the heat to low and simmer until the mixture is reduced by half, about 15 minutes.

3. Turn off the heat and stir in the lime juice and peanuts. The sauce may be served warm or cold.

Do Ahead The sauce will keep up to three days in an airtight container in the fridge.

QUICK TERIYAKI SAUCE

One of my closest friends also happens to be one of the pickiest eaters I know. Not a visit to a restaurant goes by during which she doesn't point to something on her plate and ask the server, "What. Is. This?"

When she accompanies me to a Japanese restaurant (which is so arduous for her she considers it a charitable act), she always makes a beeline for the chicken teriyaki. Frustrating as I find that, I have to admit that when done right, teriyaki is really delicious! You'll soon find that this homemade teriyaki sauce lends itself well to almost anything: seafood, chicken, beef, tofu, tempeh, or veggies. What's the trick? Let whatever you're cooking marinate in the sauce for a good long time.

This recipe makes 1 cup, but I suggest you double or even triple it so you have a batch of this awesome sauce ready to go. Serve your teriyaki chicken (or shrimp or tofu or whatever) garnished with chopped scallions and sesame seeds.

½ cup grade B organic maple syrup

½ cup tamari

½ cup rice vinegar

2 tablespoons toasted sesame oil

3 garlic cloves, minced

A 1¾-inch piece of fresh ginger, peeled and grated

1. In a small saucepan, whisk together the maple syrup, tamari, vinegar, sesame oil, garlic, and ginger. Bring to a boil over medium-high heat. Lower the heat and simmer until sauce is thickened and reduced to 1 cup, about 10 minutes.

2. Transfer the sauce to an airtight container and refrigerate until ready to use, or up to one week.

SUPERFOOD SEASONING MIX

The inspiration for this go-with-everything seasoning mixture came from the many partially used bags of nutritional seeds, herbs, and flakes that were sitting in my pantry. It became messy. Annoying. And eventually I just stopped using them.

I asked, "Why can't we just come up with a pre-blended healthy mixture to shake onto soups, salads, proteins, and whatever else we're cooking, to make it easy?" Well, here it is, folks. I'm betting you will find this mix indispensable.

If you can't find nettle flakes in the health food store, substitute nettle leaf tea: two tea bags equal 1 tablespoon. I like to use herbs and spices from the Simply Organic line.

1 tablespoon ground flax seeds
1 tablespoon toasted white sesame seeds
1 tablespoon toasted black sesame seeds
1 tablespoon dulse flakes
1 tablespoon nutritional yeast
1 tablespoon nettle flakes (optional)
1 tablespoon dried thyme
1 tablespoon dried parsley
¼ cup dehydrated kale or store-bought unseasoned kale chips, crumbled
1 teaspoon garlic powder (optional)

In a medium bowl, whisk together all the ingredients and then transfer to an airtight container.

Do Ahead The mix will keep up to one month in an airtight container at room temperature.

CHAPTER SIX

teas, juices, and smoothies

Here's a question: If a beverage could reduce your stress, sharpen your mind, boost your energy, and keep the seasonal blahs at bay, wouldn't you want to have a cup? Or three? One of the easiest and best ways to improve your health and feel your best is to try easy-to-brew teas, fresh-squeezed juice combinations, and smoothies you make at home.

Let's talk tea first. Tea is the second-most consumed beverage on the planet, just behind water. According to the Tea Association of the United States, more than 158 million Americans—about half of us—are sipping tea on any given day. And the reason is pretty simple: tea tastes good, and it's good for us. It's loaded with antioxidants, which naturally combat the aging process at the cellular level. And it's full of phytochemicals, which nutritionists believe can help reduce the risk of heart disease and cancer.

Now, to cold-pressed juices and smoothies. Yes, we are obsessed with these flavorful drinks, and the hype is real. I bet you have a Nutribullet on your counter right now (or, you have a co-worker who won't stop talking about his). The right combinations of fresh ingredients can help de-puff your eyes, curb your cravings, give you a pick-me-up when you want to reach for coffee, protect your heart, and amp up your immune system. Pulverizing the fruits, vegetables, and seeds releases all their nutrients and speed-delivers them to your body when you chug them all down.

secrets
OF THE PERFECT CUP

Few things are more therapeutic than curling up on a sofa with a hot cup of delicious tea. And while it may be easier to boil some water and toss in a tea bag, take the extra step to brew your tea using loose leaves. Most tea bags are manufactured long before they hit the store shelves, meaning the freshness of the tea could be compromised. Plus, tea bags generally contain crushed leaves rather than whole ones as found in loose teas; and when the small bits of tea leaf are exposed to light and air, their nutritional value dissipates quickly.

1. START WITH THE RIGHT WATER.
The quality of the water affects the taste of the tea, so use spring water or—if that's not available—the best filtered water you can get your hands on.

2. BOIL, SCHMOIL.
Most of us learned to bring water to a rolling boil and dunk the bag in immediately, but that's actually unnecessary. Boiling water essentially cooks the tea, which causes more tannins and caffeine to be released and can impart bitterness. Bring the water to a boil, wait a minute for it to cool down, and then steep your tea.

3. WATCH THOSE "EYES."
If you don't have a thermometer-equipped kettle, pay attention to the bubbles that form as water heats. When the bubbles start to stream upward and get larger, the Chinese refer to those as "fish eyes." For at-home brewers, that signals the water temperature is ideal— around 175° Fahrenheit.

4. BE A CLOCK WATCHER.
Steep your tea only as long as directed. More steeping doesn't lead to a better-tasting brew.

5. STAY IN THE MOMENT.
To get the most out of your tea, take your time. Respecting the process of making tea tends to create a meditative state. You're focused on the quality of the tea and the steps involved in preparing it before you even taste it.

MACA APPLE TEA

Maca has been called the "Peruvian ginseng" because taking it helps increase a person's energy levels. Professional athletes take maca powder to improve their performance. And men take it to help improve their . . . well, you know where this is going. Grown in the mountains of Peru, maca has been used by native people for centuries; it is available at your health food store, often in powder form. Its toasted oat flavor works well in this warming cider recipe. Any leftover cider will keep in the fridge for two days.

4 cups filtered water

2 cinnamon sticks

2 apple-cinnamon or apple tea bags

1 tablespoon maca powder

1 tablespoon fresh lemon juice
  (from ½ lemon)

¼ cup fresh orange juice
  (from 1 large orange)

2 teaspoons apple cider vinegar

1 teaspoon vanilla extract

1. Bring the water to a boil in a medium saucepan. Wait one minute. Remove from the heat, add the cinnamon and tea bags, and steep for 5 minutes.

2. Discard the cinnamon and tea bags. Whisk in the maca powder, lemon juice, orange juice, apple cider vinegar, and vanilla. Serve hot.

ACTIVE TIME 2 MINUTES
TOTAL TIME 8 MINUTES
SERVES 2

ACTIVE TIME 1 MINUTE
TOTAL TIME 5 MINUTES
SERVES 2

ACTIVE TIME 3 MINUTES
TOTAL TIME 7 MINUTES
SERVES 2

ACTIVE TIME 2 MINUTES
TOTAL TIME 10 MINUTES
SERVES 2

CITRUS-HIBISCUS SPICED TEA

Thank the red hibiscus flower for this tea's intense color. Not only do the anthocyanins in its petals provide a chic purple hue, but they're also potent antioxidants. Coupled with orange peel, cloves, and cinnamon, this caffeine-free brew is an anti-aging elixir.

2 teaspoons dried red hibiscus flowers
4 strips dried orange peel
1 teaspoon whole cloves
2 cinnamon sticks

1. Place the ingredients in a teapot and fill with boiling water.

2. Steep for 6 minutes or until the tea is dark purple in color; strain and pour into 2 mugs.

GINSENG ROSEBUD TEA

Ginseng is one of the most popular herbal remedies in the world. It is heralded for its ability to boost heart health, among other benefits. According to the National Institutes of Health, "ginseng has been used for treatment of heart failure and to protect tissues from damage when an organism is under stress." But don't wait for a 911 call to enjoy this complex, beautiful, and aromatic tea. You'll love how the dash of cardamom and pinch of rosebuds come together to create a fragrant, blush-colored bouquet.

4 teaspoons dried rosebuds
2 teaspoons green cardamom pods
1 teaspoon dried ginseng

1. Place the ingredients in a teapot and fill with boiling water.

2. Steep for 3 to 4 minutes, then strain into 2 mugs.

LEMON VERBENA–MATCHA BLENDED TEA

Used in Japanese tea ceremonies for centuries, matcha—that is, stone-ground green tea—is linked with improved mental health. Add some honey for sweetness, plus ginger for a kick, and this verdant drink will give you plenty to smile about.

4 teaspoons dried lemon verbena
A 1-inch piece of fresh ginger, sliced
1 teaspoon matcha powder
2 teaspoons honey

1. Place the lemon verbena and ginger in a teapot, and fill with boiling water; steep for 3 to 4 minutes.

2. Blend the matcha powder and honey to make a paste. Stir into the tea, then strain into 2 mugs.

CINNAMON APPLE ROOIBOS TEA

If you haven't tried rooibos—also known as bush tea in its native South Africa—now's the time. Whether sipped hot or enjoyed over ice, this antioxidant-rich drink is smooth and savory-sweet.

2 cups filtered water
4 dried apple rings, plus more as desired
2 cinnamon sticks, plus more as desired
2 teaspoons rooibos loose leaf tea
1 tablespoon grade B organic maple syrup (optional)

1. Bring the water to a boil in a small saucepan and remove from the heat. Add the apple, cinnamon, and rooibos; steep for 5 minutes.

2. Strain into 2 mugs and add maple syrup to taste. Serve garnished with additional cinnamon sticks and apple rings.

CIDER KOMBUCHA

Kombucha, a fizzy fermented tea drink, is absolutely teeming with probiotics—which makes this version of cider a savior for woozy, easily upset stomachs. For a stronger, more effervescent brew, refrigerate the cider in a sealed container overnight or for up to a few weeks.

½ cup unfiltered organic apple juice
2 cinnamon sticks
4 whole cloves
1 piece fresh orange peel
1½ cups unflavored kombucha

1. Bring the apple juice to a boil in a small saucepan. Remove from the heat for one minute, and add the cinnamon sticks, cloves, and orange peel. Steep for 10 minutes, then strain and set aside to cool.

2. Stir in the kombucha and serve, either hot or cold over ice.

GINGER POMEGRANATE TEA

Frequently used in Ayurvedic medicine, pomegranate is rich in vitamin C, antioxidants, and anthocyanins. It's a wellness powerhouse, made even better with the mind-sharpening qualities of fresh ginger and black tea.

2 cups filtered water
2 teaspoons black tea leaves
2 slices fresh ginger
2 tablespoons pomegranate molasses
2 tablespoons pomegranate seeds

1. Bring the water to a boil in a small saucepan. Turn off the heat, wait one minute, then add the tea leaves and ginger slices. Steep for 3 to 5 minutes, or until desired strength is achieved.

2. Strain the tea and stir in the pomegranate molasses. Serve hot, garnished with the pomegranate seeds.

DARK CHOCOLATE MATE

Finally, a hot chocolate that's actually good for you! Cacao nibs are linked to improved cardiovascular health, while yerba mate is thought to boost the immune system. Consider this your heart-healthy (and low-in-sugar) way to thrive all winter long.

2 cups filtered water
2 teaspoons yerba mate leaves
2 teaspoons cacao nibs
2 teaspoons unsweetened cocoa powder
¼ cup plain unsweetened almond milk (optional)
1 tablespoon grade B organic maple syrup (optional)

1. Bring the water to a boil in a small saucepan. Remove from the heat, wait one minute, and add the yerba mate and cocoa nibs. Steep 3 to 5 minutes.

2. Strain the tea and whisk in the cocoa powder. Add the almond milk and maple syrup (if using). Serve hot or over ice.

SWEET TURMERIC AND PEPPERED TEA

Prized for its remarkable ability to reduce inflammation, turmeric may improve joint health. This tea has plenty of the root's singularly warm flavor, along with a bit of fresh black pepper (for zing).

2 teaspoons freshly cracked black pepper
2 teaspoons grated fresh ginger
1 teaspoon ground turmeric
2 teaspoons honey

1. Combine the pepper and ginger in a teapot and fill with boiling water; steep for 3 to 4 minutes.

2. With the back of a spoon, blend the turmeric and honey to make a paste. Stir the paste into the tea then strain into 2 mugs. Serve hot.

ACTIVE TIME 2 MINUTES
TOTAL TIME 12 MINUTES
SERVES 2

ACTIVE TIME 3 MINUTES
TOTAL TIME 8 MINUTES
SERVES 2

ACTIVE TIME 2 MINUTES
TOTAL TIME 10 MINUTES
SERVES 2

ACTIVE TIME 2 MINUTES
TOTAL TIME 6 MINUTES
SERVES 2

smoothies
worth
THE SQUEEZE

If life gives you lemons, make some kind of fruit juice.
—Conan O'Brien

juicy secrets

1. DON'T THROW AWAY THE WATERMELON RIND.
Watermelon rind contains an amino acid called citrulline; it's the health and wellness world's natural answer to Viagra; it relaxes blood vessels just like the pharmaceutical drug does. Enough said! To juice the watermelon rind, simply chop it into pieces small enough to fit in your juicer. Add half a lime to punch up the flavor, if you like.

2. NO JUICER? NO PROBLEM.
Use a kitchen box grater to grate your favorite vegetables onto several layers of cheesecloth or unbleached paper towels. Wrap the fabric or paper around the grated shreds, twist tightly, and squeeze the juice into a glass. This is also a fast way to make a shot of juice if you're in a hurry and don't want to clean your appliance.

3. SOAK YOUR FLAX SEEDS.
Flax seeds have a tough outer hull that needs to be softened by soaking so they can blend right into a creamy smoothie. Place the seeds in a fine-mesh strainer and rinse them under running water to remove their enzyme inhibitors. Then, to soak, place 1 cup flax seeds (I like Bob's Red Mill) in a quart mason jar and add enough fresh cold water to cover the seeds by 2 inches. Place the lid on top, and set the jar on the kitchen counter away from direct sun for at least 12 hours and up to 24 hours. Every few days, drain off any soaking liquid, rinse the seeds, and cover them again with fresh cold water. With this method, the flax seeds will keep up to one week in the refrigerator.

4. JUICE GRAPES WITH SEEDS.
Many of the nutrients found in grapes are actually in the seeds, including essential fatty oils and antioxidants. So, when buying grapes, don't opt for the seedless varieties. Also, conventionally grown grapes can be sprayed with up to seventeen different types of fungicides and insecticides, which is why buying organic grapes is a necessity. If you can't find organic, at least go for domestically grown grapes, which tend to have less pesticide residue than grapes grown in other countries.

5. USE THE WHOLE PIECE.
Use all parts of your produce and run them through the juicer—no need to peel or core before juicing—and save your kitchen trimmings! Broccoli stems and flowering tops, beet leaves, lemon rinds, apple cores, and leftover herbs can all be run through a juicer to extract their powerful phytochemicals, vitamins, and minerals.

A SMOOTHIE FOR EVERY SEASON

I once was given a book that had more than 100 recipes just for smoothies. It was overwhelming. It was like standing in the vitamin section at the supermarket, surrounded by a nightmarishly long aisle of herbs, multivitamins, and supplements—all purported to be good for you. It's too much—and way easier just to keep pushing the cart into the next aisle and choose nothing.

This is kind of the way Costco has only one or two choices for its bulk items, like peanut butter, bed pillows, or batteries. It's as if someone did the vetting for us and said, "If you only whip up one smoothie, this is the one that's worth the effort." So, here's my all-star smoothie recipe . . . well, okay, four recipes: winter, spring, summer, and fall inspired. They are straightforward, seasonal, healthy, easy, and delicious.

WINTER SMOOTHIE
THE JEWEL OF WINTER

ACTIVE TIME 10 MINUTES
TOTAL TIME 10 MINUTES
SERVES 4

Seasonal winter fruit is a bit of an oxymoron, so this delectable, creamy smoothie depends on the protein-packed nutrition from maca, yogurt (or tofu), and milk alternatives. If you have pineapple, a few frozen chunks add the right amount of tropical goodness to help you get through the winter doldrums.

If you're making this smoothie for yourself as a meal replacement, just halve the recipe to make one generous smoothie that's a perfect breakfast or lunch.

2 cups pomegranate juice
4 apples, cored and chopped
4 tablespoons coconut sugar or honey
10 tablespoons plain Greek yogurt or silken tofu
3 cups plain unsweetened almond or coconut milk
4 teaspoons maca powder
Cinnamon, for garnish

In a blender, combine the pomegranate juice, apples, sugar, yogurt, milk, and maca powder. Blend until smooth. Serve over ice with a pinch of cinnamon sprinkled on top.

Do Ahead This smoothie can be prepared up to one month in advance: Pour the mixture into ice cube trays, cover tightly with plastic wrap, and freeze. To defrost, just place the frozen cubes into a glass and cover the top with wax paper; allow 10 to 12 hours for it to fully defrost. Stir and serve over ice.

FALL SMOOTHIE
PUMPKIN CHAI BREAKFAST

ACTIVE TIME 5 MINUTES
TOTAL TIME 6 MINUTES
SERVES 4

It's the Great Pumpkin, Charlie Brown! This is one awesome way to get your fall pumpkin fix, without the fat, guilt, or calories of pie. For an extra treat, add a dollop of whipped cream. It's still a whole lot healthier than those pumpkin spice chai whatevers you get at the chain coffee shops.

2 cups plain unsweetened almond milk, or more as needed
2 cups water
1 (14-ounce) can organic pumpkin puree
1 ripe banana, peeled
A 1-inch piece of fresh ginger, peeled
2 tablespoons grade B organic maple syrup
2 tablespoons ground flax seeds
½ cup rolled oats
1 teaspoon vanilla extract
1 teaspoon ground cinnamon
½ teaspoon ground ginger
¼ teaspoon ground cardamom
⅛ teaspoon ground cloves
3 ice cubes

Combine all the ingredients in a blender and puree until smooth. If too thick, add more almond milk. Serve immediately.

EARLY GREEN GODDESS

BERRIES 'N' GREENS

April showers bring May flowers—which means that those forgiving layers of clothing that hid the extra winter pounds will soon need to be shed. So, here's the ultimate green drink. It's loaded with vitamin-rich kale, lemon, ginger, celery, and apple—all ingredients that will put a jolt of heart- and gut-healthy reality into your system. It's also filling and can help deflate that spare tire.

You can skip the ice cubes if you store pre-cut apples, celery, and kale in an airtight container in the freezer. They'll add a chill to the smoothie without watering it down.

1 bunch kale, stems removed and leaves chopped
2 celery stalks
2 sweet apples, cored and roughly chopped
A 1-inch piece of fresh ginger, peeled
2 tablespoons lemon juice (from 1 lemon)
Zest of ½ lemon
2 tablespoons honey
2 tablespoons unrefined coconut oil
1 cup water
5 ice cubes

In a blender, combine the kale, celery, apples, ginger, lemon juice, lemon zest, honey, coconut oil, and water. Blend until smooth. Add the ice cubes and blend until frothy; add more water, if needed, for desired consistency.

Summer months usually mean long days outdoors, whether it's getting our "vitamin Sea" at the beach or hiking up the mountain for a sunrise dose of cardio. When the goal is for you and your guests to get going, and there isn't time to whip up breakfast, this is a winner. A shot of espresso and this smoothie are one of the best ways to fuel up naturally for a day in the warm Great Outdoors.

10 ounces frozen blueberries
2 cups baby kale
2 cups plain unsweetened almond milk, or more as needed
1 cup water
1 ripe banana, peeled
A 1-inch piece of fresh ginger, peeled
2 tablespoons chia seeds

In a blender, combine all the ingredients and blend until smooth. If it's too thick, add more almond milk to reach desired consistency. Serve immediately.

eat the rainbow
THE SPECTRUM OF BENEFITS

Nutritionists agree it's important to incorporate a wide variety of fruits and vegetables into your diet. There's a rainbow of nutrition that comes from adding colorful produce to your meals. That rainbow—and nutritional value—comes to us thanks to phytonutrients, the thousands of natural chemicals found in all our fruits and vegetables. Not only do phytonutrients serve as the color pigment for each of these foods, but they also provide their healthful qualities. While each of the chemicals has its own nutritional benefits and goes by different names (lycopene, beta-carotene, and resveratrol, to name a few), many if not most phytonutrients provide powerful antioxidants and may also help reduce the risk of heart disease and several types of cancers.

REDS
Great for: Circulation, lowering risk of prostate cancer, and heart and lung health
Thanks to: Lycopene, ellagic acid, catechin, anthocyanin, quercetin, and resveratrol
Good to know: Tomatoes contain loads of heart-healthy lycopene—and your body may absorb more of this phytonutrient from cooked tomatoes than fresh ones.

ORANGES
Great for: Vision, healthier skin, immune system support, easing cramps, and reducing risk of cancer and heart disease
Thanks to: Beta-carotene, alpha-carotene, and citrus bioflavonoids
Good to know: More over, carrots: when it comes to foods containing the highest level of beta-carotene—eyesight's BFF—sweet potatoes take the cake.

YELLOWS
Great for: Reducing risk of macular degeneration and cataracts; decreasing inflammation; lowering risk of skin, stomach, and breast cancers; reducing cholesterol; and aiding digestion
Thanks to: Lutein, zeaxanthin, limonoid, and bromelain
Good to know: The macula of your eye also contains lutein and zeaxanthin; they give it its yellow coloring.

GREENS

Great for: Purifying the blood, reducing cancer risk, protecting eyesight, and building stronger bones and teeth

Thanks to: Chlorophyll, vitamin K, lutein, zeaxanthin, and isothiocyanate

Good to know: In avocados and kiwis, the green pulp retains chlorophyll—an unusual thing, as the phytonutrient usually disappears in other fruits when they ripen.

BLUES & PURPLES

Great for: Memory; healthy aging; lowering cholesterol; urinary tract health; and reducing risk of cancer, stroke, and heart disease

Thanks to: Anthocyanin, resveratrol, proanthocyanidin, nasunin, and ellagic acid

Good to know: They're packed with the most antioxidants, but purple and blue foods make up just 3 percent of an average American's fruit and veg intake. Time to stock up!

Life is short.
Eat dessert
first.
—Ernestine
Ulner

CHAPTER SEVEN

sweet but not sinful treats

Did you leave room for dessert? Dessert can be our downfall at the end of a good day of healthy eating if our sweet tooth yearns for mile-high cakes and pies, whipped frostings, ooey-gooey cookies, and real ice cream swirled with fruit and caramel. And why wouldn't it? Desserts are delicious. In fact, they may be the answer to why we're all here on this great earth! To eat dessert! Marie Antoinette may have been more enlightened than we thought!

One alternative to this dilemma is to quit desserts, forever. But deprivation leads to overindulgence, which means . . . well, empty cartons of ice cream and a half-eaten sheet cake from Costco. The good news is that healthy desserts don't have to taste "healthy." When I sat down with the Natural Gourmet Institute to come up with these desserts, two things were important to me: first, the recipes must deliver some real nutritional goodness; but, second and just as important, I wanted them to be true desserts. Rich. Creamy. Crunchy. Sweet.

The Vegan Chocolate Chip Cookie Cake recipe is an all-time fave. Surprise, there are chickpeas in it—but you'd never know it when you bite into the crispy, chewy, chocolatey cookie still warm from the oven. Turn directly to page 203 to find out why this is the most *Naturally* brilliant thing, ever.

NO-BAKE COCONUT-ACAI MACAROONS

Jerry Maguire may have had you at "Hello," but this recipe had me at "No Bake." If you can't find acai powder, throw a few blueberries into the food processor instead.

⅔ cup gluten-free rolled oats

1 cup unsweetened shredded coconut

½ cup grade B organic maple syrup

2 tablespoons coconut oil, melted

2 tablespoons acai powder

1 teaspoon vanilla extract

¼ teaspoon sea salt

1. Line a baking sheet with parchment paper.

2. In a food processor, grind the oats to a flour-like texture. Add the coconut, maple syrup, coconut oil, acai powder, vanilla, and salt; pulse to combine.

3. Scoop out heaping tablespoons of the dough and place on the prepared baking sheet. Roll the dough into balls, then refrigerate until firm, about 30 minutes.

Do Ahead These no-bake macaroons can be prepared a few hours ahead and refrigerated until ready to serve. They taste best when freshly made, but because they're so easy to make, you might be tempted to call these "fast food."

Tip The difference between grade A and grade B maple syrup really comes down to taste. The "grade" here is not an indicator of quality; B just is darker, with more of a caramel taste that lends itself well to cooking and baking. But, when you buy 100 percent pure organic maple syrup, you are getting a sweetener that is free of artificial flavors or preservatives. And it's been processed by farmers who go to great lengths to protect the biodiversity of the forests where they harvest the sap for their syrup.

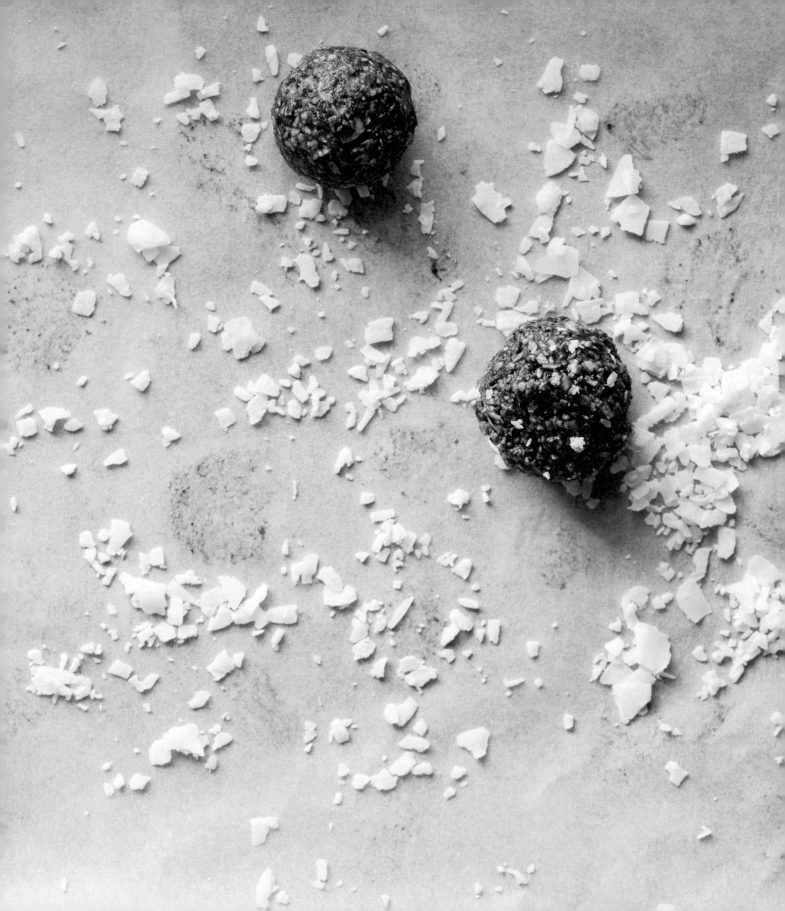

RAW COCONUT–MACA POWER POPPERS

I feel energized whenever I eat raw food. For days when the world seems to be offering more challenges than opportunities, I need the full force of every vitamin and mineral in my body. That's when raw food is my choice of fuel. These poppers refrigerate beautifully, so they are a nice pick-me-up snack in the middle of the day. In fact, if you come to the *Naturally, Danny Seo* offices, you'll likely find a Tupperware box full of them in the fridge, labeled "Don't even think about it."

½ cup plus 2 tablespoons coconut flour

3 tablespoons plus 1 teaspoon maca powder

3 tablespoons cacao powder

½ cup unsweetened shredded coconut

3 tablespoons chia seeds

⅔ cup gluten-free rolled oats

1⅓ cups raw almond, peanut, or cashew butter, at room temperature

⅓ cup grade B organic maple syrup

½ cup additional cacao powder, chia seeds, or shredded coconut (or a combination), for rolling the poppers

1. Line a baking sheet with parchment paper; set aside.

2. In a large bowl, whisk together the coconut flour, maca powder, cacao powder, shredded coconut, the chia seeds, and oats.

3. In a small bowl, stir together the nut butter and maple syrup.

4. Add the syrup mixture to the flour mixture and, using your hands, mix until thoroughly combined; you should get a firm dough.

5. Scoop the dough by rounded tablespoons onto the prepared baking sheet. Use your hands to roll each scoop into a ball.

6. Roll the balls in your choice of coating or coatings. Transfer the balls to an airtight container or enjoy at once.

Do Ahead The poppers will keep, if stored in an airtight container, in the refrigerator for up to 1 week.

Good to Know Cacao powder is raw and unprocessed, unlike the regular cocoa powder you find in the baking section of your supermarket. Look for it at natural food stores.

EASY BLUEBERRY-MASCARPONE GALETTE

Sure, supermarkets are large stores, but I think they're quite super in making our lives easier. For this galette, store-bought puff pastry is the secret to turning out a restaurant-worthy dessert. Add a scoop of whatever ice cream you want on top—the vegan Banana-Colada on page 215 or the real deal—to get that melty hot-and-cold sensation that comes only when you eat a dessert à la mode.

2 cups blueberries
¼ cup plus 3 tablespoons grade B organic maple syrup
1 cup mascarpone cheese, at room temperature
Zest of 1 lemon
1 tablespoon fresh lemon juice (from ½ lemon)
1 refrigerated pastry crust
¾ cup finely chopped raw almonds
1 large egg yolk, lightly beaten

1. In a large bowl, combine the blueberries with 2 tablespoons of the maple syrup. In a second bowl, combine the mascarpone, lemon zest, lemon juice, and ¼ cup of the maple syrup.

2. Cover your work surface with a large piece of parchment paper. Unfold the pastry dough into a 12-inch circle.

3. Spread the mascarpone filling over the dough, leaving a 1-inch border. Sprinkle the almonds over the filling, covering it evenly. Spoon the blueberries atop the mascarpone and almond mixture.

4. Using a paring knife, cut eight 1-inch slits around the edge of the dough (think of it as a clock and put slits at 12:00, 1:30, 3:00, 4:30, 6:00, 7:30, 9:00, and 10:00) and fold the edge all around toward the center. Brush the edge with egg yolk and drizzle with the remaining 1 tablespoon maple syrup.

5. Carefully transfer the parchment paper with the galette onto a baking sheet and refrigerate for 1 hour. Meanwhile, preheat the oven to 375°F.

6. Bake the galette for 45 minutes, or until the crust is golden brown and the blueberry filling is softened and syrupy.

Tip It's inevitable: blueberries stain fabrics. To remove the distinct blue stain, rub a freshly cut lemon, cut side down, all over the stain to help neutralize and "lift" it. Rinse with cold water, and blot with a clean towel to absorb as much of the stain as possible. Pour a few drops of white vinegar onto the stain as well, and then launder.

ACTIVE TIME 15 MINUTES
TOTAL TIME 1 HOUR 10 MINUTES
SERVES 8

VEGAN CHOCOLATE CHIP COOKIE CAKE

One of my earliest childhood memories is going to the mall with my mother when she ran her errands. Now as an adult, I clearly recall two things: the puppies in the window of the pet store that I desperately wanted to play with and the oversized chocolate chip cookie "cake" at the Mrs. Fields store in the food court.

This recipe is an homage to that giant cookie cake. But in our version, we lessen the fat (and guilt) by substituting chickpeas, which give the cookie a cake-like consistency but also add fiber to the delectably sweet treat. Chickpeas sound unusual here, but they are an excellent gluten-free ingredient that makes the moistest cake-like cookies and real cakes. Pour a big glass of almond milk and tear right in.

Cooking spray or melted coconut oil

2 (14-ounce) cans low-sodium chickpeas, drained and rinsed

1 cup gluten-free rolled oats

¼ cup unsweetened applesauce

3 tablespoons coconut oil, melted

2 teaspoons vanilla extract

2 teaspoons baking powder

½ teaspoon baking soda

½ teaspoon salt

1½ cups coconut sugar or turbinado sugar

1 cup fair-trade semi-sweet chocolate chips

1. Preheat the oven to 350°F. Line a 10-inch round cake pan with parchment paper and grease with cooking spray or coconut oil.

2. In a food processor, combine the chickpeas, oats, applesauce, coconut oil, vanilla, baking powder, baking soda, salt, and all but 1 tablespoon of the sugar. Puree until smooth. Using a spoon or scraper, stir in the chocolate chips.

3. Transfer the batter to the prepared cake pan and smooth the top. Sprinkle with the reserved sugar. Bake until the cake is browned around the edges but still soft in the center, about 40 minutes. Place the pan on a wire rack to cool for 15 minutes; it will firm up a bit as it cools.

4. Run a knife around the edge of the pan to release the cake. Place a large plate on top and flip to invert the cake onto the plate. Place a serving plate on top of the inverted cake and flip again so the cake is right side up. Serve warm (if you can't wait) or slice it into wedges when it has cooled.

Do Ahead The cake can be prepared up to two days in advance and kept in the fridge until ready to serve.

CHIA SEED–CACAO NIB PUDDING

I'll be honest: I was on the fence about this one. I'm a visual person, and I like our magazine stories, TV segments, and book covers to be really beautiful. When I saw this pudding sitting in the fridge, I thought it literally looked like brains. But after I reluctantly put a spoonful in my mouth, I realized you can't judge this book by its cover because this is good. Really good.

When chia seeds are combined with a liquid, they become gelatinous, making them the perfect base for a pudding. Using this shaking technique helps the seeds absorb more liquid. You'll know the pudding is ready when it is thick and custard-like. By the way, yes—chia seeds as used here are the same seeds as featured in those commercials for the Chia Pet.

2½ cups plain unsweetened almond milk

3 tablespoons grade B organic maple syrup or honey

½ cup chia seeds

1½ teaspoons unsweetened cocoa powder, or more as desired

⅛ to ¼ cup cacao nibs, plus more for garnish

1. In a 1-quart jar or container, combine the almond milk and maple syrup. Close the jar and shake well to combine.

2. Add the chia seeds, close the jar, and shake again. Add the cocoa powder and cacao nibs, close the jar, and shake yet more.

3. Refrigerate for at least 4 hours or overnight, shaking the jar every 30 minutes for the first 2 hours to prevent the chia seeds and cacao nibs from sinking to the bottom and clumping together.

4. Serve chilled, sprinkled with extra cacao nibs, if desired.

Do Ahead The pudding can be made up to three days in advance and kept in a sealed container in the refrigerator.

VEGAN CHLORELLA-MATCHA COCONUT PUDDING

The addition of chlorella to this banana and coconut pudding makes it a dessert with a big healthy punch. Chlorella is a superfood: it helps cleanse the body by removing heavy metals and toxins that may have built up in your system. It also tastes good— something like green tea. And with the sweetness from the fruit, this becomes more than just a simple pudding.

½ cup unsweetened shredded coconut

5 bananas, peeled and cut into 1-inch pieces, then frozen

8 ounces full-fat coconut milk, chilled

2 tablespoons grade B organic maple syrup

2 teaspoons matcha powder

1 teaspoon chlorella powder

½ teaspoon salt

1. In a small dry skillet, toast the coconut over medium heat, stirring constantly, until golden brown, 3 to 5 minutes. Set aside ¼ cup for the garnish.

2. In a food processor, combine the bananas, coconut milk, maple syrup, matcha and chlorella powders, salt, and other ¼ cup coconut. Puree until smooth. Transfer to a bowl, cover, and refrigerate for at least 30 minutes and up to overnight.

3. Serve the pudding topped with a sprinkle of the reserved coconut flakes.

Do Ahead Freeze the bananas and refrigerate the coconut milk the evening prior to making this pudding.

RAW COCONUT-MANGO PARFAIT

Who knew that Mary Ann's coconut cream pie, from 1960s TV's *Gilligan's Island*, was ahead of its time? Raw coconut is a fabulous addition to any dessert. Unprocessed coconut meat is a pure source of energy: when you eat it, the medium-chain triglyceride fats (the good kind) almost immediately get turned into fuel for your body.

This raw parfait is a perfect way to start the day, or to enjoy if you're planning a long bike ride or run.

1 cup packed coconut pulp and ⅓ to ½ cup coconut water (from 1 young coconut)

1 teaspoon grade B organic maple syrup

1 teaspoon vanilla extract

½ teaspoon fresh lime juice (from ½ lime)

1 cup unsweetened shredded coconut

1 mango, peeled, pitted, and cut into 1-inch cubes

1. In a blender, combine the coconut pulp and water, maple syrup, vanilla, and lime juice. Blend until smooth and refrigerate for 30 minutes.

2. Meanwhile, in a small dry skillet, toast the shredded coconut over medium heat, stirring constantly, until golden brown, 3 to 5 minutes. Transfer to a plate to cool.

3. To serve, divide the chilled coconut mixture among the serving dishes; top each with some mango and coconut.

Good to Know It's not hard to open a coconut. Many online tutorial videos show you how, but the ones you get at the supermarket are often pre-scored, making them a cinch to crack open.

PARFAIT OF FRESH BERRIES
AND VANILLA BEAN RICE PUDDING

On days when there is just *so much* going on that you literally forget to eat lunch, there is something to be said for stopping at a Chinese restaurant for takeout. The dish may not be as good as what you'd make at home, but at least you can make it a healthy choice instead of opting for greasy fast food. One bonus of Chinese takeout is the leftover cartons of rice. Redeem your moment of weakness with this oh-so-good rice pudding parfait, which transforms some leftover rice into a stunning dessert.

2 cups cooked short-grain brown rice

3 cups milk of choice

1 teaspoon ground cinnamon

1 teaspoon lemon extract

¼ teaspoon sea salt

½ cup grade B organic maple syrup

2 vanilla beans

2 cups plain Greek yogurt

½ cup hemp seeds

1 cup fresh raspberries

1 cup fresh blackberries

1. Combine the rice, milk, cinnamon, lemon extract, salt, and maple syrup in a medium saucepan. Split the vanilla beans lengthwise and scrape the seeds into the milk mixture. (Save the pods and toss them into a jar of sugar to flavor it!) Bring the milk to a simmer over medium heat and cook for 15 to 20 minutes, or until the rice has absorbed all the liquid. Let cool slightly, then fold in the yogurt.

2. Spoon some of the rice mixture into each of the serving glasses and sprinkle with some of the hemp seeds. Add a layer of berries to each glass, then repeat with more rice mixture, hemp seeds, and then berries.

3. Cover and chill the parfaits for at least 1 hour, or up to a few hours before serving.

ACTIVE TIME 25 MINUTES
TOTAL TIME 25 MINUTES
SERVES 4 TO 6

COCONUT BLACK RICE PUDDING

I have a problem with any recipe that involves cooking something slowly in the oven overnight. I don't know about you, but there's no way I can get a good night's sleep knowing the oven is on. (I can't even leave the house with the dryer going!)

Soaking some rice overnight, on the other hand, is something I feel okay about. It's a neat trick that enables you to make this awesome black rice pudding quickly.

This pudding can be topped with any of your favorite seasonal fruits, including citrus, berries, or stone fruits.

1 cup black ("forbidden") rice, soaked overnight in cold water to cover
1 (13-ounce) can full-fat coconut milk
2 teaspoons vanilla extract
½ teaspoon sea salt
1 cup water
2 tablespoons grade B organic maple syrup
½ cup unsweetened shredded coconut
2 cups chopped seasonal fruit of your choice

1. Drain the soaked rice in a strainer and rinse with fresh water. Drain again. Transfer the rice to a large pot and add the coconut milk, vanilla, salt, and water. Bring to a boil over high heat, then reduce the heat to low, cover, and simmer, stirring occasionally, until the rice is creamy and tender and most of the liquid has been absorbed, about 15 minutes.

2. Stir in the maple syrup.

3. In a small dry skillet, toast the coconut over medium heat, stirring constantly, until golden brown, 3 to 5 minutes.

4. Divide the pudding among the serving dishes; top each serving with some fruit and the toasted coconut.

Tip Before cooking rice, it's best to rinse the grains in a bowl of water to clean them. The residual water in the bowl should not be wasted; use it as a beauty treatment for your skin. The water is infused with natural plant proteins and vitamins E and B. All you have to do is soak a paper towel in the rice water, ring out the excess, and leave it on your face for 15 minutes.

BANANA-COLADA ICE CREAM

I'm a sucker for those "as seen on TV" gadgets. One day, I saw a machine that took frozen bananas and squeezed out a frozen soft-serve–consistency swirl. That was it: in go the bananas, out comes the ice cream. It seemed too good to be true until I tried this at-home version.

If you don't think vegan ice cream can taste good, you haven't tried this. To put it over the top, find a bar of good chocolate and break it into small pieces; sprinkle the bits on top for a spoonful of absolute heaven.

2 large ripe bananas, peeled and cut into 1-inch chunks (about 2 cups), frozen

1 cup frozen organic pineapple chunks

2 tablespoons cold coconut milk, or more or less as needed

2 tablespoons unsweetened shredded coconut, toasted

1. In a food processor, pulse together the bananas and pineapple, scraping down the sides as needed. It may take several minutes until the mixture transforms from chopped fruit into a creamy ice-cream–like consistency.

2. Add 2 tablespoons of the coconut milk to help the ingredients come together, adding more milk if needed; you may not need any at all.

3. Serve topped with the toasted coconut.

Do Ahead Frozen bananas will keep up to three months in an airtight container or bag. The ice cream will keep up to one month if you can restrain yourself from eating it all at once.

Tip If you love to hike or camp, healthy snacks like apples, bananas, and oranges are easy to pack along, and they carry a good dose of vitamins and natural sugar to fuel your day. But don't chuck the cores or peels into the woods. It may seem harmless, but in reality it's not that easy for these items to biodegrade all on their own, outside of a compost pile without heat or natural micro-organisms to speed the process. Apple cores can take eight weeks to break down and the peels can take up to two full years, during which time they can become eyesores and attract wild animals. Instead, pack the waste and bring them home to your compost. And by the way, chewing gum? It takes a million years to degrade.

SALTED PISTACHIO & CAULIFLOWER
ICE CREAM

If there was one recipe that best represented the mad scientist at the Natural Gourmet Institute, it would have to be this recipe. First, never in my wildest imagination would I ever think to turn a head of cauliflower into vegan ice cream. Second, never in my wildest taste buds would I ever think, "Wow, this is *really really* good." It is.

½ head cauliflower (about 1½ cups florets)
1 cup cashews, soaked and drained
1 can coconut milk
2 vanilla beans, scraped
¼ cup coconut oil
½ cup grade B organic maple syrup
½ cup brown rice syrup
1 tablespoon vanilla extract
1 tablespoon almond extract
⅛ teaspoon sea salt
½ cup pistachios, chopped, plus more
   for garnish

1. Fill a small saucepan halfway with water and bring to a boil. Cut the cauliflower into florets, add to saucepan, and cook for 5 minutes, or until tender. Drain and cool slightly.

2. Add the cooked cauliflower, cashews, coconut milk, scraped vanilla beans, coconut oil, maple syrup, brown rice syrup, vanilla extract, almond extract, and salt to a high-speed blender and process until smooth.

3. Churn the mixture in an ice cream maker according to the manufacturer's instructions. Stir in the pistachios before placing the ice cream in the freezer.

4. Serve the ice cream sprinkled with chopped pistachios.

ACTIVE TIME 30 MINUTES
TOTAL TIME 5 HOURS 30 MINUTES
SERVES 4

CELERY-CUCUMBER MINT GRANITA

I once accidentally stuck a head of iceberg lettuce in the freezer when I was in a hurry to leave for the airport. When I got back, it was as hard as a rock. (Iceberg lettuce is mostly water.) I set it on my kitchen counter to thaw, then cut it into chunks and threw it into my powerful blender to see what happened. It looked like granita, but still tasted like very, very cold lettuce.

When I mentioned the tale to our recipe developers at NGI, they giggled but realized that celery could actually make a wonderfully refreshing granita. I like when my stupid ideas turn into something good.

FOR THE CELERY SYRUP

1 celery stalk, cut into ¼-inch pieces
⅓ cup grade B organic maple syrup or coconut sugar
½ teaspoon ground celery seed

FOR THE GRANITA

4 celery stalks, cut into ¼-inch pieces
2 medium cucumbers, peeled, seeded, and diced
10 fresh mint leaves, cut into thin ribbons, plus extra for garnish
Pinch of salt

1. Make the syrup. Combine the celery, sugar, and celery seed in a small saucepan. Stir over medium heat until the sugar is dissolved. Cool to room temperature, then refrigerate until cool.

2. Strain the syrup and discard the solids. Measure ⅓ cup of the syrup for the granita.

3. Make the granita. On a parchment-lined baking sheet, arrange the celery in a single layer. Freeze until solid, about 30 minutes. (Alternatively, you can place the celery loosely into a freezer bag.)

4. In a blender or food processor, combine the frozen celery, the cucumbers, mint, reserved celery syrup, and the salt. Puree until smooth.

5. Pour the mixture into a freezer-safe 9 by 12-inch dish. Cover with plastic wrap, and place in the freezer to harden.

6. After 30 minutes, use a fork to scrape the granita, forming rough crystals. Return the pan to the freezer, and continue freezing and scraping every 30 minutes until the granita is frozen, about 4 hours. Serve the granita garnished with the remaining mint.

Good to Know Be sure the pan you use to make the granita is tempered glass or marked "freezer safe," as a regular glass dish can crack in the freezer.

Tip According to the U.S. Department of Agriculture, the average family tosses about $600 worth of groceries into the trash every year, owing to spoilage. Here's one way to stop that: if your celery stalks aren't crunchy anymore, crisp them by cutting the bottom off the stalks and placing them in a cold glass of water with a splash of white vinegar. In no time, your celery will be as good as new.

NUTTY BISCOTTI AND CARROT CAKE ICE CREAM SANDWICHES

This is the perfect summertime dessert equally for a dress-up affair (if presented on a fancy plate, of course) or for a family-friendly event in your own backyard (served on a paper napkin, instead). If you want to skip the step of making the ice cream sandwiches, know that this is just as delicious served in a dish with crumbled biscotti on top. Additionally, these sandwiches freeze well, so you'll want to make a big batch to have on hand for snacking.

1 large carrot, cut into 1-inch pieces (1 cup)

1 tablespoon coconut oil, melted

1 (14-ounce) can full-fat coconut milk

½ cup plain unsweetened almond milk

⅓ cup grade B organic maple syrup

½ teaspoon ground cinnamon

½ teaspoon ground ginger

½ teaspoon vanilla extract

Pinch of ground cloves

¼ teaspoon salt

Pinch of ground nutmeg

¾ cup chopped walnuts, toasted

1 large package store-bought almond biscotti (40 cookies)

1. Preheat the oven to 350°F. Line a baking sheet with parchment paper.

2. Place the carrot chunks on the prepared baking sheet, and toss with the coconut oil. Roast until the carrot pieces can be pierced easily with a fork, about 20 minutes.

3. Meanwhile, in a small saucepan, combine the coconut milk, almond milk, maple syrup, cinnamon, ginger, vanilla, cloves, salt, and nutmeg. Whisk until no lumps remain. Place over low heat, cover, and simmer for 10 minutes.

4. Combine the roasted carrots and milk mixture in a blender; puree until smooth. Allow mixture to cool to room temperature, about 20 minutes, then stir in the walnuts.

5. Pour the cooled mixture into an ice cream machine and freeze according to the manufacturer's directions, about 20 minutes. Transfer the ice cream to a freezer-safe container and freeze until the ice cream sets, about 1 hour.

6. To assemble the sandwiches, spread a generous dollop of ice cream on one cookie and top with a second cookie. Continue to make remaining sandwiches. Serve immediately.

Do Ahead The ice cream can be prepared up to one month in advance and kept frozen in the freezer in an airtight container.

Good to Know Instead of biscotti, these sandwiches would also work great on pizzelles.

MINT–CHOCOLATE CHIP CHEESECAKE WITH SPIRULINA

A number of recipes in this book are made with types of powdered algae. One type is chlorella (see page 206) and the other—used in this cheesecake—is spirulina. Both powders are a deep green, and either will work in this recipe. (After reading tons of research on both, I can't tell what the real difference is, other than on the molecular level, so I use them interchangeably.)

This micro algae is high in protein and nutrients like calcium, niacin, potassium, magnesium, all the B vitamins, and iron. It has a distinctive "earthy" taste that not everyone immediately embraces, so putting a little into something creamy and sweet is a surefire way to temper its strong flavor.

FOR THE CRUST

1 cup raw almonds
¾ cup dried apricots
2 tablespoons grade B organic maple syrup
2 tablespoons water
1 teaspoon vanilla extract
Pinch of salt

FOR THE FILLING

2½ cups raw cashews
⅓ cup grade B organic maple syrup
1 cup water
3 tablespoons coconut oil, melted
1 teaspoon mint extract
2 teaspoons spirulina powder
1 teaspoon vanilla extract
Pinch of salt
½ cup fair-trade finely chopped dark chocolate

1. Make the crust. In a food processor, pulse the almonds until they are the size of small peas. Add the apricots, maple syrup, water, vanilla, and salt. Pulse until the mixture begins to form a ball.

2. Transfer the dough to a 9-inch pie plate, pressing it evenly into the bottom and up the sides to form a crust.

3. Make the filling. In a food processor, combine the cashews, maple syrup, water, coconut oil, mint extract, spirulina, vanilla, and salt. Puree until completely smooth.

4. Pour the filling into the crust and freeze for 1 hour, or until ready to serve.

5. Sprinkle the cheesecake with the chopped chocolate and serve.

Do Ahead The cheesecake can be prepared up to three days ahead and kept in the refrigerator until ready to serve.

Tip One advantage of buying raw nuts over oil-roasted ones is that you know for sure your healthy snack is free of GMOs. Often, nuts are roasted in soybean or canola oils, which are more likely to have been made from GMO-developed plants.

FLOURLESS DOUBLE-CHOCOLATE CAULIFLOWER BROWNIES

No, this is not a sneaky nod to Jessica Seinfeld's hidden vegetable recipes (although, it definitely could work!). Gluten-free brownies, which omit flour, tend to be a bit dense. The addition of cauliflower here is a nutritional boost, but also helps give the brownies a cake-like quality.

½ head cauliflower (about 1½ cups florets)

½ cup organic milk, at room temperature

1 cup fair-trade bittersweet chocolate chips, melted

½ cup butter, melted (plus more to grease pan)

3 organic eggs

½ cup grade B organic maple syrup

1 cup pecans, ground

¾ cup coconut flour

½ cup unsweetened cocoa powder

2 teaspoons cinnamon

½ teaspoon baking powder

⅛ teaspoon sea salt

1. Preheat oven to 350°F. Grease an 8-inch square baking pan and set aside.

2. Add the cauliflower and milk to a high-speed blender and puree until smooth. Add in the melted chocolate, butter, eggs, and maple syrup, and blend until combined.

3. In a medium bowl, combine the ground pecans, coconut flour, cocoa powder, cinnamon, baking powder, and salt.

4. Gently fold the wet ingredients into the dry ingredients. Pour the batter into the prepared pan and bake for 30 to 40 minutes, or until firm to the touch. Cool before slicing.

ACKNOWLEDGMENTS

THE *NATURALLY, DELICIOUS* TEAM:

Armando Rafael

Eugene Jho

Nidia Cueva

Alexis Cook

Bridget Collins

Christopher Stone

Janine Desiderio

Stacie Stukin

Jonathan Rheingold

AT NATURAL GOURMET INSTITUTE:

Jacqueline Somen

Alexandra Shytsman

Susan Baldassano

Tracy Koy

Cara Lanzi

Olivia Roszkowski

AT PENGUIN RANDOM HOUSE:

Pam Krauss

Nina Caldas

Ian Dingman

Claire Vaccaro

Justin Thrift

Erica Rose

Casey Maloney

Farin Schlussel

AT *NATURALLY, DANNY SEO* MAGAZINE:

Ben Harris

Stanley Harris

Kara Sloman

Janet Mowat

Jodi Zucker

Wojtek Urbanek

Sandra Soria

Christine Richmond

Amy Feezor

Jasmine Chang

And all of our incredibly talented writers, photographers, and stylists who make the pages of my magazine look so beautiful.

AT DANNY SEO MEDIA VENTURES:

Joy Tutela

Maggie Dumais

Megan Brown

Matt Lefferts

Tom Carr

Steven Pregiato

Rich Pedine

Jenny Heller Giagni

Noelle Primavera

AND A BIG THANK-YOU TO MY FRIENDS AT:

Wilsonart

Bosch Home Appliances

Padilla CRT

APA

Tremendous Entertainment

Litton Entertainment

CBS Television

INDEX

ABOUT THE AUTHOR

Danny Seo is the editor in chief of *Naturally, Danny Seo*, a national print magazine that celebrates the idea that style and sustainability don't need to be mutually exclusive from each other.

He is also the host of the upcoming TV show *Naturally, Danny Seo*, which brings all of the ideas for cooking, home decorating, beauty, wellness, and travel to life that you see in the pages of his magazine.

Naturally, Delicious is his tenth book and his first cookbook.

In addition, Danny's line of branded eco-friendly products are sold in stores across the United States, Canada, and Europe and includes retailers such as TJ Maxx, Marshalls, and HomeGoods.

Danny lives in Bucks County, Pennsylvania. You can follow him on Instagram and Twitter @DannySeoMag and learn more at DannySeo.com.

ABOUT NATURAL GOURMET INSTITUTE

Founded in 1977 by Annemarie Colbin, PhD, Natural Gourmet Institute (NGI) is the leader in health-supportive culinary education. Natural Gourmet Institute's Chef's Training Program is a comprehensive and professional program that trains students to meet the growing demand for culinary professionals who are able to make the connection between food and health. NGI's interactive and dynamic Certificate Programs are designed to give students firsthand experience and expertise in the areas of Culinary Nutrition, Cooking for People with Illness, Writing for Food Media, Raw and Living Foods, Food Entrepreneurship, and Sustainable Farming. Natural Gourmet Institute also offers public intensives, hands-on instruction, demonstrations, and lectures for the healthy cooking enthusiast. On Friday night, the school is transformed into an intimate dining room, where Chef's Training Program students and instructors prepare a three-course plant-based dinner that is innovative, delicious, and beautifully presented.

Learn more at: www.NaturalGourmetInstitute.com.